THE JIIM DOMAIN: EXAMINATION OF U.S. MILITARY SUSTAINMENT ASSISTANCE FOLLOWING NORTH KOREAN REGIME COLLAPSE

ABSTRACT

THE JIIM DOMAIN: EXAMINATION OF U.S. MILITARY SUSTAINMENT
ASSISTANCE FOLLOWING NORTH KOREAN REGIME COLLAPSE, by MAJ
Edward K. Woo, 163 pages.

The United States of America has and continues to have a long-standing adversarial
relationship with North Korea. As Presidential administrations turn over, the U.S. policy
on North Korea remains largely unchanged due to North Korea's unpredictable, volatile,
and oftentimes erratic behavior as perceived from a global premise over the past 60 years.
This condition exists because of the dictatorial regimes of Kim Jong Un and his
predecessors. North Korea isolates itself from the rest of the global community through
the auspices of communist ideals and provocations that led to damaging ties with its
neighbors. North Korea's provocations historically have led to hunger, famine,
malnutrition, and violation of human rights. The purpose of this qualitative case study
analysis is to determine how the U.S. and Republic of Korea militaries sustain and
support a North Korean regime collapse using data triangulation and purposeful sampling
to base North Korea against three other case studies. The significance of the relationship
is that it may inform the audience of how the current sustainment architecture on the
peninsula can dependably support the Republic of Korea as in the best political,
economic, and strategic interests of the U.S. This research is significant in relation to the
vision of the President of the United States in his strategic military rebalance towards the
Pacific.

ACKNOWLEDGMENTS

First and foremost, I give thanks and gratitude to God.

I would like to thank my wife, Youngmi, for her patience, support, and understanding through the process. I would like to thank my mother, Stacey, who brought me up with confidence, self-determination, and a focus on studying. I would also like to acknowledge my father, Charles, and my brother, Kenneth, for instilling intellectual stimulation at an early age. I want to say a special thank you to my curious son Justin for always asking me what I am doing while pecking away at the keyboard.

I wish to thank several friends and colleagues for their interest in, and stimulating discussion of, many of the issues dealt with in this thesis. They include Dr. O. Shawn Cupp, Mr. John Ukleya, and Mr. Neal H. Bralley for the long hours they spent proofreading drafts and providing valuable feedback. Without candor, dedication, and stewardship, this thesis would fail to materialize. I especially would like to thank my committee chairperson, Dr. Cupp, for the expert guidance and facilitation he provided; he kept me focused and grounded on a product that is relevant and timely. Of the aforementioned, I respect their desire to help hard-pressed students gain the benefits in thought-provoking projects such as this.

TABLE OF CONTENTS

ACRONYMS

ASCC	Army Service Component Command
CFC	Combined Forces Command
CIRH	*Commission Interimaire pour la Reconstruction d'Haiti*
CJTF-HOA	Combined Joint Task Force- Horn of Africa
C-SPT	Commander for Support
DMZ	Demilitarized Zone
DPRK	Democratic People's Republic of Korea (North Korea)
EACTI	East Africa Counterterrorism Initiative
EPLF	Eritrean People's Liberation Front
EPRDF	Ethiopian People's Revolutionary Democratic Front
ESC	Expeditionary Sustainment Command
ETM	Essential Tasks Matrix
EUSA	Eighth U.S. Army
HBCT	Heavy Brigade Combat Team
ICTY	International Criminal Tribunal for the former Yugoslavia
IDPs	Internally Displaced Persons
IFOR	Implementation Force
IGO	Intergovernmental Organizations
ISB	Intermediate Staging Base
JIACG	Joint Interagency Coordination Group
JIIM	Joint, Interagency, Intergovernmental, and Multinational
JTF	Joint Task Force
KTO	Korean Theater of Operations

LOGCAP	Logistics Civil Augmentation Program
MINUSTAH	United Nations Stabilization Mission in Haiti
NATO	North Atlantic Treaty Organization
NGO	Non-Governmental Organization
NSE	National Support Element
OSCE	Organization for Security and Co-operation in Europe
OUR	Operation Unified Response
PLS	Palletized Load System
POL	Petroleum, Oils, and Lubricants
PVO	Private Voluntary Organization
RAND	Research and Development Corporation
ROK	Republic of Korea
SFOR	Stabilization Force
UN	United Nations
UNHCR	United Nations High Commissioner for Refugees
UNPA	United Nations Protected Areas
UNPROFOR	United Nations Protection Force
USAFRICOM	United States Africa Command
USAID	United States Agency for International Development
USAREUR	United States Army Europe
USCENTCOM	United States Central Command
USEUCOM	United States European Command
USFK	United States Forces Korea
USPACOM	United States Pacific Command
USSOUTHCOM	United States Southern Command

ILLUSTRATIONS

TABLES

CHAPTER 1

INTRODUCTION

North Korea will achieve nothing by threats or by provocations. North Korea knows its obligations, and it must take irreversible steps to meet those obligations. On this, the United States and the Republic of Korea are absolutely united. . . . It is none of our interests to see either tension and instability in the region [or to see] a nuclearized peninsula.[1]

— President Obama

U.S. government planners are no strangers to analyzing armed conflicts and regional instability. The majority of planners will profess that there is no simple formula to solve the intricacies of post-conflict reconstruction. These types of deliberations oftentimes induce an unwieldy and complex environment interlaced with parallel threads, ambiguous relationships, inter-relationships, and national and institutional affinities in a multiplex of dynamic ecosystems.[2]

The United States of America has and continues to have a long-standing adversarial relationship with North Korea. As presidential administrations turn over, the U.S. policy on North Korea remains largely unchanged because of North Korea's unpredictable, volatile, and oftentimes erratic behavior over the past 60 years. The U.S. presidential administration aims to exercise multilateral pressure on North Korea to relinquish its nuclear option.[3] This condition exists because of the dictatorial regimes of Kim Jong Un and his predecessors. North Korea isolates itself from the rest of the global community through the auspices of communist ideals and provocations that led to damaging ties with its neighbors. North Korea is adept at employing military provocations and brinksmanship tactics.[4] North Korea's provocations historically have led to hunger, famine, malnutrition, and violation of human rights.

1

This research is significant in relation to contemporary threats in the Pacific and how the President of the United States refocuses diplomatic, military, information, and economic strategic balance towards the region. In the Pacific theater of operations lie the Korean peninsula and its sustainment challenges. Sustainment lessons learned from other campaigns in history could assist the sustainment of forces in the Korean peninsula. This assistance will include number and types of units, types of equipment, doctrine, plans, combined sustainment, and institutional sustainment. Understanding the impact of North Korean regime collapse and retaliation with North Korean forces will also enable future officers to better articulate sustainment needs and requirements of the future force. This articulation is necessary during interaction among soldiers, sailors, airmen, Marines, the U.S. Department of Defense, and other government agencies with centralized initiatives to refocus on the Pacific theater.

The Quadrennial Defense Review of 2010, the National Security Strategy of 2013, the National Military Strategy of 2011, the *Sustaining U.S. Global Leadership: Priorities for 21st Century Defense of 2011* document, and the Chairman's Strategic Direction to the Joint Forces of 2012 underscore an emphasis on the Asia-Pacific. In theory, these strategic documents provide purpose to the global employment of the force with a sustainment force package right-sized, developed, trained, and maintained. This thesis highlights circumstances in history of other countries when the military was not ready as the military sustainment posture was one of the reasons for this lack of readiness. The research specifically addresses how planners employ and strategize the elements of sustainment in potential North Korean regime collapse.

2

The elements of sustainment include logistics, personnel services, financial services, and health services support that enable success in operations by providing military forces operational reach and freedom of action. This study will not attempt to solve in totality the entire regime collapse, but will attempt to alleviate and placate the demand signals that yield the sustainment capabilities in the Korean theater of operations (KTO). This thesis is limited to the KTO but addresses its impacts in its area of interest. The following list describes key terms as part of this thesis.

Key Terms

Airfield. An area prepared for the accommodation (including any buildings, installations, and equipment), landing, and takeoff of aircraft.[5]

Area of Interest. An area of interest is "that area of concern to the commander, including the area of influence, areas adjacent thereto, and extending into enemy territory to the objectives of current or planned operations if those objectives are not currently within the assigned operational area. This area also includes areas occupied by forces or other factors that could jeopardize the accomplishment of the mission."[6]

Area of Responsibility. "The geographical area associated with a combatant command within which a geographic combatant commander has authority to plan and conduct operations."[7]

Army Service Component Command. "Command responsible for recommendations to the joint force commander on the allocation and employment of Army forces within a combatant command."[8]

Ballistic Missile. "Any missile which does not rely upon aerodynamic surfaces to produce lift and consequently follows a ballistic trajectory when thrust is terminated."[9]

Brigade Combat Team. "A combined arms team that forms the basic building block of the Army's tactical formations."[10]

Combatant Command. "A unified or specified command with a broad continuing mission under a single commander established and so designated by the President, through the Secretary of Defense and with the advice and assistance of the Chairman of the Joint Chiefs of Staff."[11]

Crisis. "An incident or situation involving a threat to the United States, its citizens, military forces, or vital interests that develops rapidly and creates a condition of such diplomatic, economic, or military importance that commitment of military forces and resources is contemplated to achieve national objectives."[12]

Demilitarized Zone. "A defined area in which the stationing or concentrating of military forces, or the retention or establishment of military installations of any description, is prohibited."[13]

Disarmament. "The reduction of a military establishment to some level set by international agreement."[14]

Distribution. "The operational process of synchronizing all elements of the logistic system to deliver the right things to the right place at the right time to support the geographic combatant commander."[15]

Host-Nation Support. "Civil and/or military assistance rendered by a nation to foreign forces within its territory during peacetime, crises or emergencies, or war based on agreements mutually concluded between nations."[16]

Intergovernmental Organization. "[17]An organization created by a formal agreement between two or more governments on a global, regional, or functional basis to protect and promote national interests shared by member states."

Internally Displaced Person. "Any person who has been forced or obliged to flee or to leave their home or places of habitual residence, in particular as a result of or in order to avoid the effects of armed conflict, situations of generalized violence, violations of human rights or natural or human-made disasters, and who have not crossed an internationally recognized state border."[18]

Joint. Connotes activities, operations, organizations, etc., in which elements of two or more Military Departments participate.[19]

Joint Logistics. Joint logistics is "the coordinated use, synchronization, and sharing of two or more Military Departments' logistic resources to support the joint force."[20]

Joint Logistics Operations Center. "The current operations division within the Logistics Directorate of the Joint Staff, which monitors crises, exercises, and interagency actions and works acquisition and cross-servicing agreements as well as international logistics."[21]

Joint Logistics Over-the-Shore Operations. "Operations in which Navy and Army logistics over-the-shore forces conduct logistics over-the-shore operations together under a joint force commander."[22]

Logistic Support. "Support that encompasses the logistic services, materiel, and transportation required to support the continental United States-based and worldwide deployed forces."[23]

Logistics. "Planning and executing the movement and support of forces."[24]

Maneuver. "Employment of forces in the operational area through movement in combination with fires to achieve a position of advantage in respect to the enemy."[25]

Materiel. All items (including ships, tanks, self-propelled weapons, aircraft, etc., and related spares, repair parts, and support equipment, but excluding real property, installations, and utilities) necessary to equip, operate, maintain, and support military activities without distinction as to its application for administrative or combat purposes.[26]

Multinational. "Between two or more forces or agencies of two or more nations or coalition partners."[27]

Multinational Logistics. "Any coordinated logistic activity involving two or more nations supporting a multinational force conducting military operations under the auspices of an alliance or coalition, including those conducted under United Nations mandate."[28]

National Support Element. "Any national organization or activity that supports national forces that are a part of a multinational force."[29]

Noncombatant Evacuation Operations. "Operations directed by the Department of State or other appropriate authority, in conjunction with the Department of Defense, whereby noncombatants are evacuated from foreign countries when their lives are endangered by war, civil unrest, or natural disaster to safe havens as designated by the Department of State."[30]

Nongovernmental Organization. "A private, self-governing, not-for-profit organization dedicated to alleviating human suffering; and/or promoting education, health care, economic development, environmental protection, human rights, and conflict resolution; and/or encouraging the establishment of democratic institutions and civil society."[31]

Nonproliferation. "Actions to prevent the proliferation of weapons of mass destruction by dissuading or impeding access to, or distribution of, sensitive technologies, material, and expertise."[32]

Operational Reach. "The distance and duration across which a joint force can successfully employ military capabilities."[33]

Reception. "The process of receiving, off-loading, marshalling, accounting for, and transporting of personnel, equipment, and materiel from the strategic and/or intratheater deployment phase to a sea, air, or surface transportation point of debarkation to the marshalling area."[34]

Refugee. "A person who, owing to a well-founded fear of being persecuted for reasons of race, religion, nationality, membership of a particular social group, or political opinion, is outside the country of his or her nationality and is unable or, owing to such fear, is unwilling to avail himself or herself of the protection of that country."[35]

Supplies. In logistics, all materiel and items used in the equipment, support, and maintenance of military forces. See also component; equipment.[36]

Supply point distribution. "A method of distributing supplies to the receiving unit at a supply point. The receiving unit then moves the supplies to its own area using its own transportation."[37]

Sustainment. Sustainment is the provision of logistics, personnel services, medical services, and financial services necessary to maintain and prolong operations until successful mission completion.[38]

Theater of Operations. "An operational area defined by the geographic combatant commander for the conduct or support of specific military operations."[39]

Unity of Effort. "Coordination and cooperation toward common objectives, even if the participants are not necessarily part of the same command or organization, which is the product of successful unified action."[40]

Assumptions

A North Korean regime collapse will trigger an attempt by Kim Jong Un to employ belligerent DPRK enemy combatants south of the Demilitarized Zone (DMZ) against Combined Forces Command (CFC) and United States Forces— Korea (USFK). Over time, CFC and USFK will respond to a humanitarian aid effort of three million internally displaced persons (IDPs) or refugees coming into the ROK.[41] One other key assumption is that the North Korean threat to the Republic of Korea (ROK), its neighbors, and U.S. forces in the region is serious. This thesis highlights, in relative detail, the nuclear option of North Korea. Nevertheless, one final key assumption is that North Korea will not employ nuclear weapons.

Limitations

The research considering the breadth and depth of the U.S. Army sustainment capabilities will encounter a myriad of challenges. Because of the grand scope of the KTO, this thesis does not completely address other variables (such as terrain, weather, media, and support for other organizations) because of time constraints. Thus, this thesis harbors limitations that are significant to appreciate and grasp the basic problem and does not allow the thesis to grow untenable. Sustainment capabilities in the Korean peninsula to support a combined joint operation will prove its utility during current and future administration so long as North Korean provocations are extensive.

Delimitations

One service branch that is not included in this thesis paper is the U.S. Coast Guard. This thesis does not address diplomacy and contingency plans. The Essential Tasks Matrix as used in this thesis limits to five general technical sectors and lacks the level of detail into 1,178 individual tasks. The commodities or classes of supply included in this manuscript are water, food, fuel, and medical supplies. This thesis does not include other classes of supply. The manuscript includes considerations of South Korean government's capabilities to provide sustainment services during North Korean regime collapse, but does not go into specific detail.

Background

Despite North Korea's volatile behavior over several decades, the transfer of command from father to son in the midst of a struggling economy and extensive hunger was seamless.[42] After the seamless transition in December 2011, Kim Jong Un appears to have an active stranglehold on North Korea. The answer to why studying a DPRK regime collapse is important is multifold. North Korea has a disastrous centralized economy, decrepit industrial sector, deficient agricultural base, underfed military and populace, and budding nuclear programs.[43] The chances of a sudden leadership change in the North could prove destabilizing and unpredictable. A sparsely prepared response to regime collapse can lead to serious consequences and the prospect of broader warfare.

As the political, diplomatic, economic, and social atmosphere changes in the Asia-Pacific, the focus to study the sustainment capabilities is significant in the Korean peninsula. The concept of maneuver will be difficult to negotiate through the uncompromising terrain of the Korean peninsula and flow of IDPs moving to the South. Moreover, a sustainment architecture that befits all quantifiable and doctrinal metrics to support the concept of maneuver is a daunting, albeit obligatory task for any sustainment planner to forecast in the KTO.

This matter centers on the concept of maneuver and the numbers of sustainment units and equipment that can support the number of divisions and brigades in theater. The thesis assertion is how the U.S. military could successfully conduct sustainment operations during the North Korean Regime Collapse. The significance of the relationship is that it informs the audience of the current sustainment architecture on the peninsula. The analysis also enables planners to determine how to dependably support and sustain the Republic of Korea in the best political, economic, and strategic interests of the U.S.

The North Korean Threat

Various analysts describe the North Korean threat ranging from terms such as marginal, unrealistic, petty, dangerous, catastrophic, and very serious. Despite the wide range of opinions, the U.S. official stance on the North Korean threat is "the North Korean military poses a serious threat to the ROK, its other neighbors, and U.S. forces in the region."[44]

A multinational Joint Civilian Military Investigation Team summarized North Korea's motives based on key events of the last four years. The team concluded that the

10

"North Korean midget submarine conclusively sank the ROK naval corvette . . . killing 46 ROK sailors. . . . North Korea shelled Yonpyong Island, killing two ROK Marines and two civilians."[45] Policymakers cannot underscore calculated attacks on the ROK, as North Korea possesses an ambitious ballistic missile development program and mobile theater ballistic missiles capable of reaching targets throughout the Pacific theater.[46]

The North Korean threat includes a ground military force structure that contains an infantry corps, a mechanized infantry corps, an armor corps, and an artillery corps with 4,100 tanks, 2,100 armored vehicles, and 8,500 field artillery platforms.[47] With the strength of nearly one million troops, North Korea's ground forces comprise of the vast majority of its military. North Korea hedges their antiquated conventional weapon systems based on 1970s technology with an abundance of artillery platforms and augmenting its light infantry force.

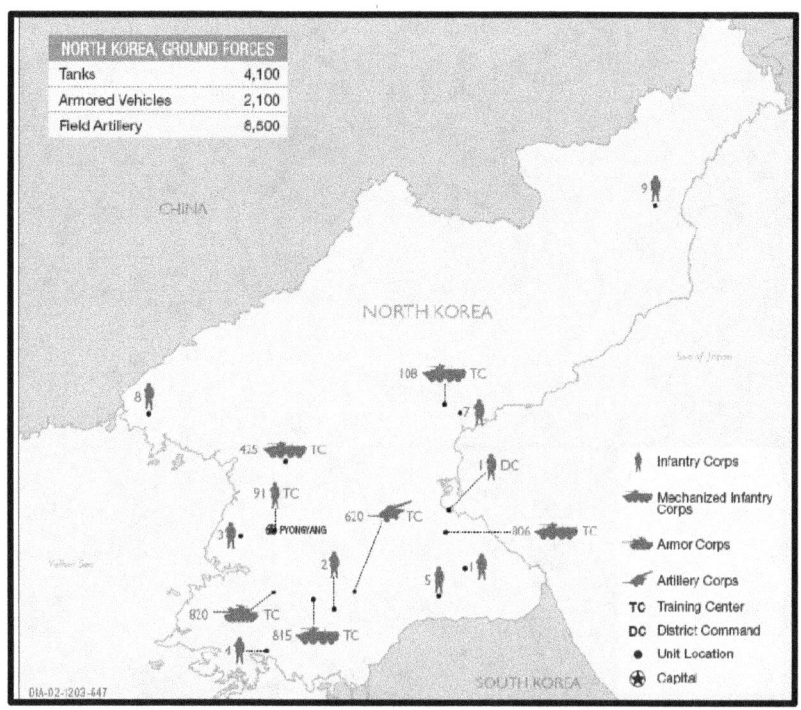

Figure 1.   North Korean Ground Forces Data

Source: Data from U.S. Office of the Secretary of Defense, *Military and Security Developments Involving the Democratic People's Republic of Korea (A Report to Congress Pursuant to the National Defense Authorization Act for Fiscal Year 2012)* (Washington, DC: Government Printing Office, 2012), 11.

The North Korean air forces consist of 92,000 personnel with 730 sorties of combat aircraft, 300 helicopters, and 290 transport aircraft.

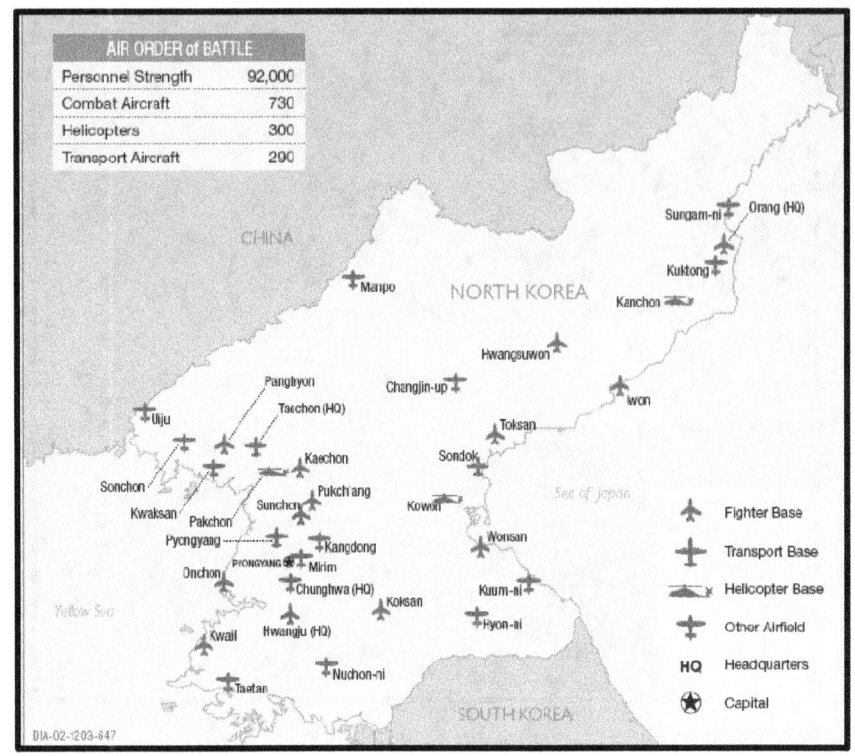

Figure 2.   North Korean Air Forces Data

Source: Data from U.S. Office of the Secretary of Defense, *Military and Security Developments Involving the Democratic People's Republic of Korea (A Report to Congress Pursuant to the National Defense Authorization Act for Fiscal Year 2012)* (Washington, DC: Government Printing Office, 2012), 13.

The North Korean naval forces consist of 60,000 personnel with 70 submarines, 420 patrol combatants, 260 amphibious landing craft, 30 mine warfare vessels, and 30 support or auxiliary vessels.

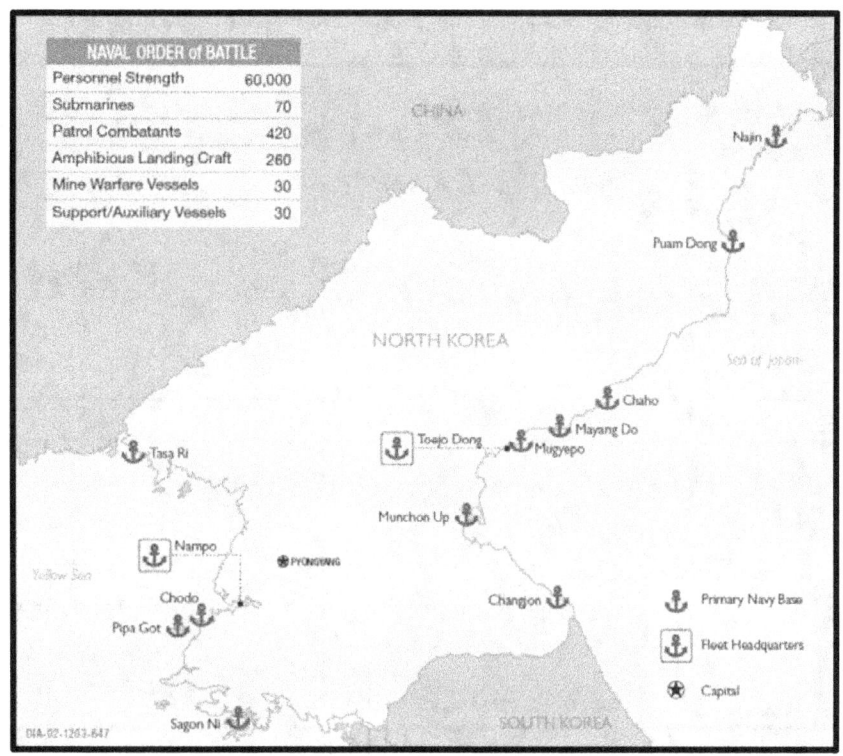

Figure 3.   North Korean Naval Forces Data

Source: Data from U.S. Office of the Secretary of Defense, *Military and Security Developments Involving the Democratic People's Republic of Korea (A Report to Congress Pursuant to the National Defense Authorization Act for Fiscal Year 2012)* (Washington, DC: Government Printing Office, 2012), 14.

Of the North Korean military capabilities, perhaps its most critical asset is its ballistic missile force. North Korea has an aggressive ballistic missile program and exported platforms to countries such as Iran and Pakistan.[48] North Korea has produced its own versions of the SCUD B and SCUD C (an extended-range version of the SCUD B).[49] North Korea will continue employing and improving the Taepodong-2, which could reach the United States with a nuclear payload if developed as an intercontinental ballistic missile.[50]

Table 1.   North Korea, Ballistic Missile Forces

System	Launchers	Estimated Range
KN-2	Fewer than 100	75 miles
SCUD-B		185 miles
SCUD-C		310 miles
SCUD-ER		435-625 miles
No Dong	Fewer than 50	800 miles
IRBM	Fewer than 50	2,000+ miles
TD-2	Not yet deployed	3,400+ miles

Source: Data from U.S. Office of the Secretary of Defense, *Military and Security Developments Involving the Democratic People's Republic of Korea (A Report to Congress Pursuant to the National Defense Authorization Act for Fiscal Year 2012)* (Washington, DC: Government Printing Office, 2012), 15.

Nuclear Weapons Proliferation

On 25 May 2009, North Korea conducted a nuclear test detected by at least 61 seismic stations.[51] United States containment of nuclear proliferation predates to the Truman doctrine, where George Kennan outlined the nuclear prospects of the Soviet Union. The U.S. acquired unique skills to enhance containment efforts over the past few decades.[52] "In November 2010, the DPRK showed visiting experts early construction of a 100 Megawatt-Thermal light-water reactor and a newly built gas centrifuge uranium enrichment plant, both at the Yongbyon site."[53]

Photo Removed Due to Copyright Restrictions

Figure 4. North Korean Missile Threats

Source: John Lloyd, "North Korea's Known Unknowns," Reuters, April 8, 2013, http://blogs.reuters.com/john-lloyd/2013/04/08/north-koreas-known-unknowns/ (accessed February 6, 2014).

A few years later in February 2013, the North Korean news agency reported a prosperous underground detonation resulting in an earthquake of 5.1 magnitude.[54] These tests affirm North Korea's commitment to arm the warheads for long-range attacks.[55] Despite these provocations, little is known regarding the specificities or sophistication of the North Korean nuclear warhead design.

Current estimated plutonium stocks in North Korea's inventory amass to 30 kg and 50 kg or enough plutonium for approximately five to eight nuclear weapons.[56] Furthermore, North Korea possesses a distinguished size and sophistication of highly enriched uranium plants.[57] After the Six-Party talks, North Korea stalled pre-coordinated and anticipated denuclearization talks in February 2012. "Concerns persist that North Korea will continue its proliferation of missile and nuclear technology for a variety of motivations, including financial profit, joint exchange of data to develop its own systems, and as part of the general provocative trend."[58]

Threat to Stability

U.S. officials describe the North Korean nuclear program fit more for deterrent operations, international prestige, and coercive diplomacy than for war fighting.[59] The Congressional Research Service Report on North Korea also stipulates that North Korea will likely use nuclear weapons only as a last option when perceived to be on the verge of military defeat or "irretrievable loss of control."[60]

U.S. National Security Strategy

The U.S. security strategy outlines the strengthening of the Nuclear Non-Proliferation Treaty as the foundation of nonproliferation to hold nations like Iran and North Korea accountable for their failure to meet international obligations.[61] The document stipulates that the U.S. will pursue denuclearization not to single out nations, but to proceed on a path to enhanced political and economic integration with the international community."[62] If North Korea ignores their international obligations, the U.S. will pursue any means to increase their isolation and bring them into compliance with nonproliferation norms.[63]

---

[1]Jennifer Epstein, "Obama Warns North Korea," Politico, March 25, 2012, http://www.politico.com/news/stories/0312/74434.html#ixzz2jF5IMeET (accessed November 11, 2013).

[2]Ryan Whalen, "The U.S. Government as an Interagency Network," *Interagency Journal* 4, no. 1 (Winter 2013): 75.

[3]National Committee on American Foreign Policy, "North Korea," *American Foreign Policy Interests* 29, no. 1 (2007): 88, http://dx.doi.org/10.1080/ 10803920601188201 (accessed October 17, 2013).

[4]Peter M. Beck, "North Korea in 2010," *Asian Survey* 51, no. 1 (February 2011): 33, http://dx.doi.org/10.1525/as.2011.51.1.33 (accessed October 17, 2013).

[5]U.S. Joint Chiefs of Staff, Joint Publication 1-02, *Department of Defense Dictionary of Military and Associated Terms* (Washington, DC: U.S. Joint Chiefs of Staff, March 15, 2014), 7.

[6]U.S. Joint Chiefs of Staff, Joint Publication 3-0, *Joint Operations* (Washington, DC: U.S. Joint Chiefs of Staff, April 11, 2011), IV-1.

[77]U.S. Joint Chiefs of Staff, *Department of Defense Dictionary of Military and Associated Terms*, 17.

[8]Ibid.

[9]Ibid., 23.

[10]Ibid., 29.

[11]Ibid., 41.

[12]Ibid., 61.

[13]Ibid., 70.

[14]Ibid., 75.

[15]Ibid., 77.

[16]U.S. Joint Chiefs of Staff, Joint Publication 4-0, *Joint Logistics* (Washington, DC: U.S. Joint Chiefs of Staff, October 16, 2013), GL-6.

[17]U.S. Joint Chiefs of Staff, *Department of Defense Dictionary of Military and Associated Terms,* 134.

[18]Ibid., 135.

[19]Ibid., 139.

[20]Ibid., I-2.

[21]Ibid., 146.

[22]Ibid.

[23]Ibid., 161.

[24]Ibid.

[25]Ibid., 163.

[26]Ibid., 166.

[27]Ibid., 178.

[28]Ibid.

[29]Ibid., 183.

[30]Ibid., 187.

[31]Ibid., 188.

[32]Ibid., 189.

[33]Ibid., 196.

[34]Ibid., 221.

[35]Ibid., 223.

[36]Ibid., 252.

[37]U.S. Department of the Army, Field Manual 4-40, *Quartermaster Operations* (Washington, DC: U.S. Department of the Army, October, 2013), 2-2.

[38]U.S. Joint Chiefs of Staff, *Department of Defense Dictionary of Military and Associated Terms,* 255.

[39]Ibid., 266.

[40]Ibid., 276.

[41]Bruce W. Bennett, *Preparing for the Possibility of a North Korean Collapse* (Santa Monica, CA: Rand, 2013), 68.

[42]Peter M. Beck, "North Korea in 2011," *Asian Survey* 52, no. 1 (February 2012): 65, http://dx.doi.org/10.1525/as.2012.52.1.65 (accessed October 17, 2013).

[43]Bennett, *Preparing for the Possibility of a North Korean Collapse*, 68.

[44]U.S. Office of the Secretary of Defense, *Military and Security Developments Involving the Democratic People's Republic of Korea (A Report to Congress Pursuant to the National Defense Authorization Act for Fiscal Year 2012)* (Washington, DC: Government Printing Office, 2012), 8, http://www.defense.gov/pubs/report_to_ congress_on_military_and_security_developments_involving_the_dprk.pdf (accessed January 29, 2014).

[45]Ibid.

[46]Ibid., 9.

[47]U.S. Office of the Secretary of Defense, *Military and Security Developments Involving the Democratic People's Republic of Korea*, 11.

[48]Ibid., 15.

[49]Ibid.

[50]Ibid.

[51]Jonathan Medalia, *North Korea's 2009 Nuclear Test: Containment, Monitoring, Implications* (Washington, DC: Congressional Research Service, November 24, 2010), 1.

[52]Ibid., 1.

[53]Mary Beth Nikitin, *North Korea's Nuclear Weapons: Technical Issues* (Washington, DC: Congressional Research Service, April 3, 2013), 1.

[54]Ibid.

[55]Ibid.

[56]Ibid., 4.

[57]Ibid., 8.

[58]Ibid., 28.

[59]Ibid., 18.

[60]Ibid.

[61]The White House, *National Security Strategy* (Washington, DC: The White House, May 2010), 4.

[62]Ibid., 23.

[63]Ibid., 24.

CHAPTER 2

LITERATURE REVIEW

North Korea . . . with its bellicose rhetoric, its actions, has been skating very close to a dangerous line. Our country is fully prepared to deal with any contingency, any action that North Korea may take or any provocation that they may instigate.[1]

— Secretary of Defense Chuck Hagel

To comprehend North Korea's motives, one may explore the chronology of events over time leading to the ideology North Korea exudes today and the events that led to its disposition in world events. Korea has a comprehensive cultural history of roughly five thousand years.

Korean History and Atmospherics

North Korea has a deep-seeded resentment towards world politics. This section provides the socio-political framework to explain North Korea's interpretation of the global domain. This literature review will outline sample dynamics from the Sino-Japanese War, Russo-Japanese War, Japanese Rule of Korea from 1910-1945, the Korean War, and contemporary times. From a historical standpoint, Korea acted as a platform of numerous global struggles and proxy wars among dominant actors in international politics.

The Sino-Japanese War of 1894-1895

Qing Dynasty China and Meiji Japan fought over Korea control during the Sino-Japanese War of 1894-1895. Japan succeeded in blocking Chinese influence over Korea. Some historians view the Sino-Japanese war as the genesis of the modern disputes over the control of Korea because of its attractive location of surrounding littorals as avenues to impact global trade through port control. Some historians and researchers view the Sino-Japanese War as the genesis of the deep-seeded animosity between Japan and Korea. Japan originally intended to aid Korea, but ultimately assassinated Korea's Queen Min. "Japanese officers had her hacked to death in her palace on 8 October 1895 . . . the Koreans never forgave the Japanese for the murder of their queen."[2]

The bilateral dynamics of Japanese assassination of Korea's Queen Min provoked mistrust and deceit in due course. Russia maneuvered their position to gain port control around Korea during the Sino-Japanese War. Russia also reaped benefits because of Japan's successful obstruction of Chinese influence. "The real struggle . . . did not concern China but was between Russia and Japan."[3] Because of competing geopolitical interests, Japan and Russia engaged each other during the Russo-Japanese conflict.

The Russo-Japanese War of 1904-1905

The conclusion of the Sino-Japanese War between China and Japan resulted in a clash of imperial powers for Korea control between Japan and Russia. Russia's enormous investment in the Manchurian railway concessions in the years concluding the Sino-Japanese War precipitated the Russo-Japanese War.[4] Japan witnessed Russia's attempt at procuring East Asian railways as a strategic effort to deter Japan's imperialistic domination and hegemonic efforts.

Diplomatic campaigns to settle Korea into two spheres of influence proved unsuccessful that led to the first major war of the 20th century. The Japan and Russia negotiations eventually faltered and the competition for dominance evolved into the Russo-Japanese War in 1904.[5] Japan stunned the global world by thwarting Russian influence as one of the first victories over a great Western power. A Japanese victory placed them in a commanding position to dominate the Korean peninsula. U.S. President Theodore Roosevelt encouraged representatives to end the Russo-Japanese War under the auspices of the Treaty of Portsmouth.

In the war's aftermath, President Roosevelt's complicity of Japanese domination over Korea helped shape modern Korean beliefs and values system in the global realm. President Roosevelt oftentimes encouraged Japanese domination of Korea while preferring the Japanese over the Koreans, sometimes viewing Koreans in utter contempt.[6] Korea was in the position as an overlooked state in the middle of powerful imperial nations. Overlooked and frustrated, this shaped the beginning of Korea's strategy of self-reliance.

Korea from 1910-1945

After Japanese victory in the Russo-Japanese War, Korea petitioned multiple times for the U.S. to intervene and adhere to previous treaty commitments to Korea. However, Syngman Rhee, leader of the Korea independence movement from Japan, unsuccessfully petitioned the U.S. during the Roosevelt and Wilson Presidential administrations as the U.S. disregarded the petitioners.[7] The U.S. perception of Japan as the de facto power over Manchuria infuriated Korean nationalists and imbalanced any peaceful equilibrium to a condition of misery, betrayal, and repression.

Rhee again attempted unsuccessfully thwarting Japan colonization of Korea during the 1921-1922 Washington Conference. In desperate pursuit of freedom, Koreans saw in Chinese Communism the hope to end the turmoil. The history behind Japanese treatment of Korean comfort women set the conditions for bitter strife between the two parties and fueled the mentality of dissension and search for a new system of government. During the conflicts in the Asia Pacific during the 1930s and 1940s, the Japanese government mobilized hundreds of thousands of Asian women, many of them Korean, to military brothels to serve Japanese soldiers.[8]

Furthermore, after Japan surrendered in 1945, the international tribunals did not prosecute Japan's actions as a war crime; this oversight indicated that the situation was a form of legalized military rape of the subjected women.[9] The absence of an official Japanese apology further embittered relationships between Japan and Korea. As a result, the future leaders of Korea, who were young men at this time, developed an agenda not to trust any other nation.

Korea from 1945-1950

The Japanese surrendered to the Allies to end World War II. This also ended Japanese colonization. Korea became a divided nation in 1945 when at the Potsdam Conference, allies decided to divide Korea without ever consulting Rhee or any Koreans. After independence from Japan, Russia and China involved themselves in conversations with Kim Il Sung, North Korea's future leader. This period began with Russia and China ensconced to the north of the 38th parallel while the U.S. secured the South. At the time, the dividing line of the two Koreas was temporary. However, the added effect of the Cold War exacerbated the situation that led to the Korean War.

After many years of negligence, the U.S. recognized the Republic of Korea as the official government of the South. By 1950, most Korean communists seceded from power to either Rhee in the South or Kim Il Sung in the North. On June 25, 1950, North

Korea breached the 38th parallel to invade the South, officially beginning the Korean War. Kim Il Sung's vision was to unite the two Koreas.

The Korean War from 1950 to 1953

The Korean War became one of the most horrific events in modern history. The Cold War aggravated the internal civil war in Korea. On the allied forces spectrum, "the United States insisted that the division agreed upon with the Russians in 1945 to separate the North from the South at the 38th parallel had, in fact, created two separate and subsequently independent nations."[10] Nearly two million Koreans died in the war. The Korean War was probably the single most dangerous moment of the Cold War and Korea constituted a potential flashpoint in superpower rivalry.[11]

Cold War territorial disputes commenced in Korea and while nations like Russia, China, and the U.S. overlooked the Korean War (some calling it the Forgotten War), the two Koreas never forgot. The two Koreas experienced hundreds of thousands of civilian killings and underscored painful memories for Koreans. North Korea required the lives, property, and obedience of its constituents for the state's own survival under unavoidable circumstances.[12] The Korean War was a proxy war for global superpowers as Kim Il Sung capitalized on Russia's Marxist-Leninist ideals to solidify his own form of government for his people.

Korea from 1953 to 1994

The end of the Korean War solidified sovereign lines between North and South Korea. By most economic measures immediately after the partition, North Korea was relatively stronger in terms of industry and natural resources. After 1953, the two Koreas developed in very different directions. One adopted Stalin's approach as the North's economy boomed and the South was a basket case that inculcated capitalism.[13] After over thirty years of industrial development, the Soviet Union fell in 1989 at the end of the Cold War.

Without Soviet aid, North Korea experienced an unsustainable economy, which at its worst, led to a famine that killed three million North Koreans. After Kim Il Sung died in July 1994, North Korea witnessed the rise of Kim Jong Il. Kim Jong Il believed that even though North Korea was a small territory, he could stabilize the nation and create a powerful and prosperous country by growing the military.[14] Kim Jong Il witnessed North Korea's military revolution and used extortion techniques as North Korea's primary global policy instruments. This period heightened North Korea's Juche ideology and shaped its agenda to remain as secretive as possible to the rest of the world. To remain secluded from the rest of the world was a major part of the Juche ideology.

In the midst of global denigration and socio-economic defamation, in the 1990s, North Korea embraced the opportunity of nuclear technology. South Korea experienced the First Republic of South Korea from 1948 to 1960 followed by the Korean Second Republic for eight months. After the Korean war, South Korea witnessed the eviction of Rhee and the rise of Park Chung-Hee, a military general that executed a successful coup d'état in 1961.

South Korea's economy was troubled but saw growth and development in the 1960s, where some historians credit Park Chung-Hee for instigating an economic revival. The South Korean economy grew rapidly during the Third and Fourth Republics. "In the process of the geopolitical and geo-economic transformations of the early post-Cold War

27

years, a highly asymmetric Beijing-Pyongyang-Seoul triangular economic relationship has emerged"[15]

How did North Korea Become an Impoverished Warrior State?

The Fifth Republic of Korea saw the end of military influence and the Sixth Republic of Korea in 1987 generated leaders elected by popular vote. Since 1987, South Korea's relationship with the United States blossomed where North Korea adopted a Juche ideology inhabited by the previous century's amalgam of despair, turmoil, and grief. "The notion of Juche . . . started to develop in the mid-1950s during [a] dispute with the Soviet Union [and] formed the ideological basis of Kim Il Sung's totalitarian system"[16] Juche ideology is independence or self-reliance derived primarily from the Marxist-Leninist theory based on a very strong cadence of nationalism.[17] Other factors contribute to the Juche ideology such as trauma from embittered Japanese colonial rule and arrogance of communist allies to impose their development models onto North Korea.

Originally, Kim Il Sung adopted Maoist ideas, such as the idea of self-regeneration in the 1950s and 1960s. Juche was the foundation of the Five-Year Plan of 1956-1961, also known as the Chollima Movement, which led to numerous reforms in North Korea. The goal of the Five-Year Plan was swift economic progress for North Korea with a large industrial base. The Soviet Union had a marked impact on North Korea's plans as it mirrored the Soviet Union's Five Year Plan in 1928. The relationship between the Soviet Union and North Korea was real and substantiated by partnership and open communication. After the time of the Sino-Soviet conflict in 1972, Juche replaced

Marxism-Leninism in the revised North Korean constitution as a result of the Sino-Soviet split.

The Marxist-Leninist roots were indispensable in the creation of Juche. After the 1991 collapse of the Soviet Union, North Korea's greatest economic partner, Marxism-Leninist ties with Juche was dropped in North Korea's constitution as Kim Jong-Il incorporated the Songun (army-first) policy into Juche in 1996.[18] Over time, North Korea's economic stance as part of the communist bloc precipitated on the world stage. As global and economic partners diminished coupled with the self-reliance tenets of Juche that acquiesced to overconfidence and stubbornness, North Korea matriculated into an impoverished warrior state.

Photo Removed Due to Copyright Restrictions

Figure 5.   Contributing Factors to Juche Ideology

Source: Figure graphics created by author. Content derived from Han S. Park, ed., *North Korea: Ideology, Politics, Economy* (Englewood Cliffs, NJ: Prentice Hall College Div, 1996), 53.

South Korea's Developing Policies and Economic Trends from 1990 to Present

South Korea suffered in 1997 through what is commonly referred to as the International Monetary Fund crisis. South Korea's banking sector suffered from non-performing loans as its large corporations funded aggressive expansions such as Kia Motors and Hyundai Corporation. Hasty expansions of conglomerates worsened the South Korean economy to compete on the world stage. Many businesses failed and excess debt led to major takeovers. In the wake of the Asian market downturn in November 1997, Moody's lowered the credit rating of South Korea from A1 to A3. The Seoul stock exchange fell 7 percent.

The South Korean dropped from 1,700 per U.S. dollar to 800 per U.S. dollar. Despite this weak economic time, South Korea's economy rapidly increased and swiftly overcame the financial crisis in 1997 and returned to a flourishing economy by 2006. Today, the ROK enjoys strong diplomatic ties, enhanced information capabilities, and highly technical industries. The South Korean president Kim Dae-Jung, from 1998 to 2003, sparked reconciliation efforts with Kim Jong Il but made little progress.

Recently, North Korea's Kim Jong Il died in February 2011. His heir, Kim Jong Un, became the de facto supreme leader of North Korea. "Six decades have passed since the outbreak of the war, and yet sporadic fighting continues in spite of the armistice agreement. The remains of too many soldiers lie buried and forgotten, and war wounds of too many survivors remain unrecognized and unhealed."[19]

Impending North Korean Regime Collapse

The DPRK is a failing state, having economic instability and unable to provide proper nutrition to its constituents.[20] Starvation is commonplace. "North Korea is experiencing lots of rebellious behavior in the forms of refugee flows into China, major black market activities, graft and corruption by DPRK authorities, and even reported attacks on North Korean leaders."[21]

China is North Korea's only treaty ally and provides the impoverished North Korea with half of its sustenance, three-quarters of its trade, and virtually all of its crude and refined oil. China's relationship with North Korea mirrors oppositely with the U.S. relationship with South Korea. North Korea's memory of the western world of the Sino-Japanese War, Russo-Japanese War, Japanese colonization during 1910-1945, and the Korean War is fresh and remains antagonistic. "Relations between North Korea and Japan in the postwar era have fluctuated over time, from moves toward reconciliation to reversion, to tension."[22]

North Korea's focus on nuclear proliferation is evident as North Korea demands, "to be recognized as nuclear-armed. In response, the United States and its Asian allies have signaled that North Korea cannot expect business as usual."[23] Economic instability and socio-political volatility initiate a progressive nature for a North Korea regime collapse. North Korea employs nuclear threats as extortionist tools to survive in a sophisticated global economy. "There is thus an imperative to use all tools of persuasion to stop North Korea's nuclear-development program before it becomes more deadly."[24]

North Korea's circular and unceasing approach to influence provocations for humanitarian aid is a strategy without lasting confidence and fidelity. Without a full

31

diplomatic resolution, North Korea will fall into an imploding series of events that will include various actors and non-state actors to swarm South Korea in an impending, complex, and erratic operational conditions. "Neither a North Korea backed into a corner, nor forced regime change, will serve the region or the world well. The consequences of either of these outcomes for the people of North Korea would be brutal."[25]

Despite numerous claims for non-aggression, DPRK provocations remain prominent. In 2013, the DPRK claimed that the U.S. is the sworn enemy of the Korean people with further provocations of nuclear strikes and testing. "Nearby nations are waiting to see whether and how well Kim consolidates his power base, the expected alternative being domestic instability in North Korea."[26] Prison camps are abundant in North Korea as a psychological instrument to control population and belief systems. North Korean propaganda induces a nationalistic atmosphere for North Korean leaders.

A regime collapse is imminent from a diplomatic, informational, military, social, and economic standpoint. Several experts predicted a regime collapse over the past decade, but North Korea remains sovereign. In 2014, a regime collapse study is crucial because of the shifting priorities of the U.S. security policy towards the Asia-Pacific. Furthermore, the implications of U.S. policy for potential Korea unification have other results to include the intervention of China, Russia, and Iran.

A change in regime will stimulate an economic revolution in East Asia, albeit a catastrophic one. "Reform of the North Korean economy would have two profound effects: first, there would be a significant increase in exposure to international trade . . . second, changes in the composition of output could be tremendous, involving . . . millions of workers changing employment."[27]

As long as diplomatic, military, and economic turbulence occurs in North Korea, U.S. military professionals should remain alert and plan for the right amount of responsive support under the enemy's most likely course of action. In Joint Publication 4-0, sustainment is "the provision of logistics and personnel services necessary to maintain and prolong operations until successful mission completion. Sustainment in joint operations provides the Joint Force Commander flexibility, endurance, and the ability to extend operational reach.[28] Because of the interplay of armed conflict and refugee assistance, planners pursue an effective sustainment plan to determine how the commander can seize, retain, and exploit U.S. interests and initiatives.

Most Likely Courses of Action

"Because the interplay between North Korea and Northeast Asia is highly complex and even confusing, fraught with paradoxical expectations and consequences, there is no single or simple answer."[29] Because of the convoluted nature of these events, this paper relies on assumptions to control the research of North Korean regime collapse. An assumption based on the literature review is that a North Korea regime collapse will induce internally displaced persons across the 38th parallel and into South Korea. Militarily, North Korea will invade South Korea by means of force, while highly trained Republic of Korea military, backed by allies will be ready to defend. Three million internally displaced persons and refugees will move towards the South to rekindle relationships with lost family members. The underpinnings of erratic operational conditions lead to an unwieldy force structure to promote the peace and stability of the Republic of Korea.

Most Dangerous Course of Action

The most dangerous course of action in a North Korean regime collapse is a last effort to launch weapons that can produce mass destruction. As evidenced in the following figures illustrating North Korean missiles and their slight, albeit plausible nuclear capabilities, an employment of a revenge attack using nuclear weapons is not impossible. The use of a nuclear weapon is the most dangerous course of action as "North Korea might threaten a nuclear attack on a city like Pusan if ROK/U.S. forces cross the DMZ or approach Pyongyang as part of a counteroffensive, and execute that threat if ROK/U.S. forces still advance."[30] A delivered and reliable 10-kiloton nuclear weapon burst in Seoul could cause 125,000 to more than 200,000 fatalities and 290,000 to more than 400,000 fatalities and casualties combined.[31]

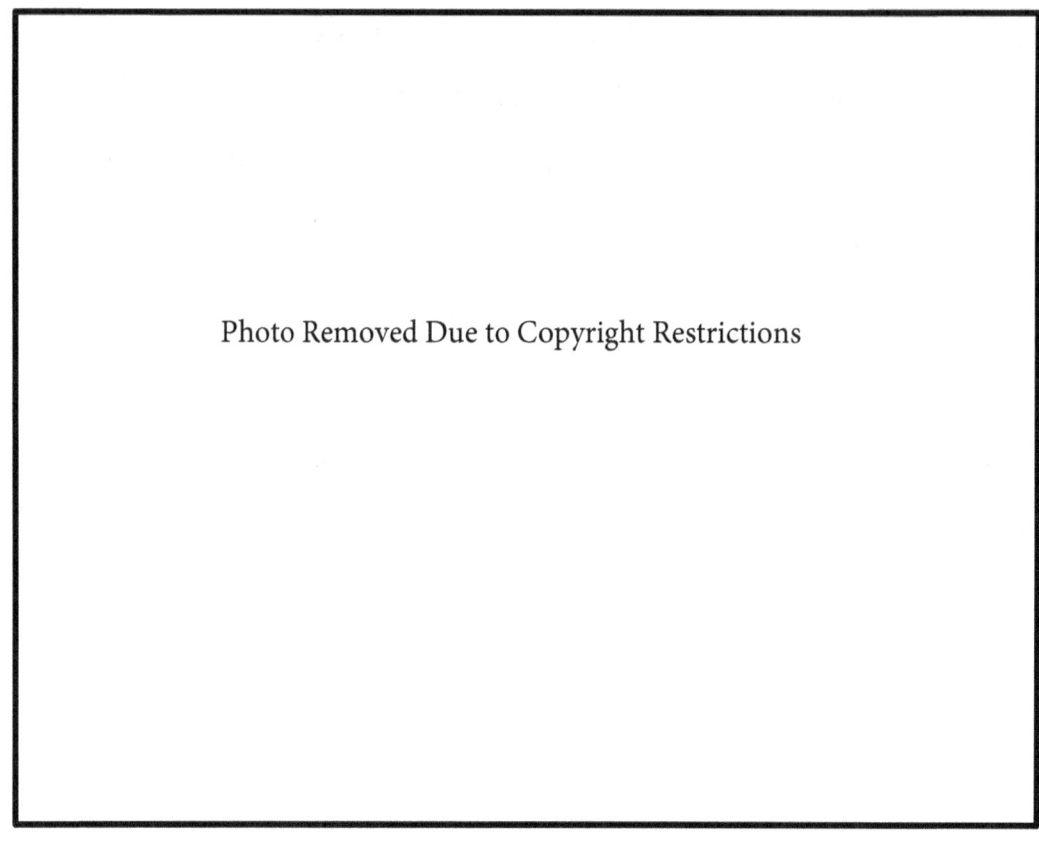

Figure 6.   North Korea's Missile Program

Source: BBC News, "North Korea's Missile Programme," April 12, 2013, http://www.bbc.co.uk/news/world-asia-17399847 (accessed February 7, 2014).

Economically, "considering only primary and secondary effects, the Korean gross domestic product might be reduced by at least 10 percent for ten years or more, amounting to a cost of roughly $1.2 trillion. The ROK wealth might be reduced by perhaps 4 percent, or $120 billion."[32] The nearly $1.5 trillion loss to the ROK economy is plausible and will deal damage to infrastructure, organic industrial capability, and government operations. The U.S. governs the nuclear umbrella guarantee for the ROK and Japan to employ its arsenal in response to North Korean antagonism.

35

Notwithstanding, ROK and Japan likely will develop independent capabilities in the event of a North Korean nuclear attack.

Photo Removed Due to Copyright Restrictions

Figure 7. Locations of North Korean Nuclear Sites

Source: BBC News, "North Korea's Missile Programme," April 12, 2013, http://www.bbc.co.uk/news/world-asia-17399847 (accessed February 7, 2014).

Themes in Literature Review and Synthesis

The central theme of the literature review posits a climate of conflict over the past several centuries. The U.S. military has experience because of involvement in the Korean

War and maintains a presence on the peninsula. Germane to the problem statement, researchers require an intensive analysis of diplomatic, informational, military, and economic variables based on the aforementioned literature review with contemporary military joint doctrine. Fusing historical vignettes with present-day military capabilities will underscore solutions and implications for further research.

Sustainment Architecture and Analysis

Over the course of several decades, the U.S. military presence on the Korean peninsula dwindled to fewer than 20,000 U.S. military personnel. Correspondingly, the U.S. sustainment architecture decreased because of reduced capacity and budget. The U.S. currently operates an expeditionary sustainment command with a wide variety of assets. Many other key organizations supplement the command to include an Army Field Support Brigade, supply centers, transportation control centers, maintenance units, distribution units, and port activities. The current structure supports the current U.S. force but operates in combined environment with a similarly structured sustainment command belonging to the ROK military.

The expeditionary sustainment command headquarters operates on the peninsula whereas the theater sustainment headquarters is not; the higher headquarters operates in Hawaii and supports the entire U.S. Pacific Theater of operations. The higher sustainment command is a theater sustainment command that enables the sustainment execution of contingency on the Korean peninsula. The sustainment organizations on the peninsula are in practice for numerous decades, participating in conferences, combined exercises, training events, and multinational cooperation activities with allied nations.

Overarching the sustainment commands are senior staff proponents of the CFC and USFK, a four-star command dedicated to the military operations in Korea. The senior logistics officer is a one-star general who oversees logistic planning activities in conjunction with the sustainment command general officer in charge. Together, the leadership conjoins complex military planning through doctrine, organizations, training, materiel, leadership, education, personnel, and facilities.

All sustainment planners aim to support the USFK mission during armistice, crisis, and contingencies through policy management and procedures for transportation, munitions, petroleum, logistics readiness and planning, mortuary affairs, maintenance, and medical. More importantly, sustainment planners incorporate ROK partners to prepare, coordinate, and negotiate international agreements, minimizing costs, and Wartime Host Nation Support with the ROK government representatives.

Terrain is one of the variables that remain constant because of its geographic nature. It takes several hundred years to witness minute shifts in natural terrain to include mountains, valleys, rivers, and lakes. Terrain is a factor to understand defensive and offensive military strategy and its implications. Notes on terrain from several decades past are relevant today. In an excerpt from a "Logistics Study of the Korean Campaigns: 1950-1953," the Eighth United States Army Logistic Chief (G4) "quickly learned that in a mountainous country having as primitive a state of road development as Korea, the standard means of transportation to front line units envisioned by army doctrine was inadequate."[33] Fehrenbach (2001) also observed sustainment planning in stating "a war can no more be successfully fought without political concerns for the future than a panzer can roll without gas"[34]

The same manuscript from the Eighth United States Army G4 called for "more extensive study [to] be made of the problem of supplying front line troops in mountainous terrain, with a view toward providing organic means of transport for units."[35] Shortly after Operation Chromite, General MacArthur set up a centralized logistical command to support the KTO during the Korean War.[36] The U.S. logistical support to the United Nations allies during the Korean War was one of the extreme logistical missions in history.

During the 1950s, the only principal port in South Korea was the port of Pusan.[37] The mountainous terrain of Korea adds to security issues and the "inflexibility and vulnerability of transportation."[38] "In Korea, the operational logistics system sustained the Naktong (Pusan) Perimeter, the Inchon landing, and the ground offensive into North Korea."[39] A lack of a sustainment plan and architecture was the critical lesson learned from the outset of the Korean War. "One of the more glaring deficiencies in the Korean War was the absence from the beginning of a prepared plan for logistical support of operations in Korea."[40] After the conclusion of the Korean War, most of the sustainment deficiencies during the Korean War disappeared with a prolonged U.S. presence on the peninsula for over fifty years.

Despite the myriad of improvements, challenges remain. "Within the Korean theater for the last 20 years, there have been significant inefficiencies and complexities that have contributed to redundancies and competition for scarce resources."[41] The subsequent decades allowed the U.S. to raise not only its own joint sustainment architecture, but also the one of the Republic of Korea. The key to sustainment planning is improvement of South Korea's road networks, port facilities, and airfields. North

Korea's infrastructure is relatively stagnant from the conclusion of the Korean War, with roads "built for the most part . . . unpaved [with] steep curves and steep grades, particularly in the mountainous areas, further [restricting] the highway net."[42] During North Korean regime collapse, U.S. and R.O.K. units may engage in kinetic and humanitarian aid operations above the border entering a dilapidated road network that presents significant sustainment risk. Military sustainment planners analyze a logistics challenge by class of supply. The classes of supply enable measuring excess or shortfalls based on daily requirements and organic capabilities.

CLASSES AND SUBCLASSES OF SUPPLY		
Symbol Classes	**Description**	**Subclasses**
☾ CLASS I	Rations	A - Nonperishable C - Combat Rations R - Refrigerated S - Non-Refrigerated W - Water
CLASS II	Individual Equipment & General Supplies	A - Air G - Electronics B - Ground Support Material M - Personal Weapons E - General Supplies T - Industrial Supplies F - Clothing
CLASS III	Fuel, POL	A - POL for Aircraft W - POL for Surface Vehicles P - Package POL
CLASS IV	Engineer & Barrier Material	A - Construction B - Barrier
CLASS V	Ammunition	A - Air Delivery W - Surface Weapons
CLASS VI	Sundry, Personal Demand	A - Personal Demand P - Ration Supplementary M - Mail, Personal & Official Sundry Pack
CLASS VII	Major End Items	A - Air / Aviation L - Missiles B - Ground Support Material M - Weapons D - Administrative Vehicles N - Special Weapons J - Tanks, Packs, Adaptors, & T - Industrial Material Pylons (USAF) X - Aircraft Engines
CLASS VIII	Medical Supplies	A - Medical Material, including medical peculiar repair parts B – Blood/ Blood Products
CLASS IX	Repair Parts	A - Air L - Missiles B - Ground Support Material M - Weapons D - Administrative Vehicles N - Special Weapons
CA CLASS X	Material for Nonmilitary Programs	G - Electronics T - Industrial Material K - Tactical Vehicles
LEGEND: **POL** = Petroleum, Oil, and Lubricants // **USAF** = United States Air Force		

Figure 7. Classes and Subclasses of Supply.

Source: U.S. Department of the Army, Field Manual 4-95, *Logistics Operations* (Washington, DC: U.S. Department of the Army, April 2014), 1-7.

A military sustainment planner anticipates, by class of supply, the prospect of consumption values based on educated planning factors based on daily requirements measured in short tons, flat racks, or other distribution capabilities. For example, a military sustainment planner who anticipates a brigade of 3,947 persons who consume class I (water) of 6.1 gallons per person per day has to figure 24,076.7 gallons of water per day. Sustainment planners also consider whether purified water or packaged (bottled) water is more appropriate.

Typically, a hybrid solution of both bulk potable and packaged water challenges the military sustainment planner to analyze distribution methods with the capability organic to a distribution company. A distribution company can transport bulk potable water on Load Handling Systems or packaged water on Palletized Loading Systems. A distribution company has a robust inventory to adequately distribute supplies to its organic brigade. The challenge lies in sustaining internally displaced persons where the U.S. government typically charges the military, as the first responder, to provide sustainment support to initiate stability operations.

A military unit may or may not be able effectively to sustain a military force or stability operation based on planning factors and daily requirements. Planners that identify a shortfall have a responsibility to identify shortfalls and raise the issue to higher headquarters and figure out a solution for the maneuver force to extend operational reach, prolong endurance, and sustain momentum.

The table below highlights the logistic situation of one U.S. Army heavy brigade combat team (HBCT) and its logistic situation. This table outlines the forecasted supply consumption and distribution necessary to sustain a HBCT in an offensive operation

(which satisfies the first of two assumptions, the second being IDPs).

Table 2.   Logistics Situation of an HBCT

Class of Supply	Planning Factor	Daily Requirement	Capability	Excess / Shortfall
I	3 x Meals/ Person/Day	11,841 Meals/Day 10.83 STONs/Day 20.56 Pallets/Day	Stores, Issues, Distributes at Field Ration Issue Points	94.966 STONs excess capability; no shortfalls
Water (Bulk)	0.907 Gallons/ Person/Day	3,580 Gallons/Day	Stores and distributes 32,000 gallons to 4 forward support companies	28,420 gallons excess capability; no shortfalls.
Water (Packaged)	3.34 Gallons/ Person/Day	12,183 Gallons/Day 45.49 STONs/Day 49.8 Pallets/Day	Distributes up to 105.79 STONs/Day	60.3 STONs excess capability; no shortfalls
III(B)	1,362 Gallons/ Truck Company/Day	31,227 Gallons/Day	Distributes up to 69,500 Gallons/day	38,273 gallons excess capability; no shortfalls
VIII	.19 Pounds/ Person/Day	750 Pounds/Day 0.397 STONs/Day 1.13 Pallets/Day	Distribute up to 105.79 STONs/Day	105.393 STONs excess capability; no shortfalls
The planning factor for the brigade combat team is 3,947 personnel. The Operational Readiness Rate is 93 percent, which assumes 7 percent of the U.S. military equipment is unable to conduct sustainment operations.				

Source: Created by author.

The next table outlines the second assumption of three million internally

displaced persons in North Korea. The DPRK's population as of 2010 is roughly 25

million people.[43] Large numbers of starving persons will have an impact of Class I

requirements, but the thesis controls this to the standard three meals per person per day.

Table 3.   Logistics Situation of Three Million IDPs

Class of Supply	Planning Factor	Daily Requirement	Capability	Excess / Shortfall
I	3 x Meals/ Person/Day	9,000,000 Meals/Day		Shortfall; The U.S. Military will require an additional 15 Transportation Medium Truck Cargo Companies (40-Ton)
		8,232 STONs/Day		
		15,628 Pallets/Day		
Water (Bulk)	0.907 Gallons/ Person/Day	2,721,000 Gallons/Day		Shortfall; The U.S. Military will require an additional 65 Quartermaster Water Purification and Distribution Companies or 12 Transportation Medium Truck Cargo Companies (40-Ton) with Compatible Water Tank Racks
Water (Packaged)	3.34 Gallons/ Person/Day	30,060,000 Gallons/Day	Organic military support companies or non-divisional truck companies	Shortfall; The U.S. Military will require an additional 114 Transportation Medium Truck Cargo Companies (40-Ton) or 103 Transportation Medium Truck Companies (PLS) (Local Haul)
		112,241 STONs/Day		
		122,876 Pallets/Day		
III(B)	1,362 Gallons/ Truck Company/Day	386,808 Gallons/Day		Shortfall; The U.S. Military will require one Transportation Medium Truck Company (POL) (7,500 gallons)
VIII	.19 Pounds/ Person/Day	570,000 Pounds/Day		Shortfall; The U.S. Military will require one additional Transportation Medium Truck Cargo Company (40-Ton)
		302 STONs/Day		
		859 Pallets/Day		
Notes: There is one non-divisional transportation company on the KTO. The planning factor for the IDPs is 3 million personnel. The Operational Readiness Rate is 93 percent, which assumes 7 percent of the U.S. military equipment is unable to conduct sustainment operations.				

Source: Created by author.

These tables act as planning factors to incorporate fidelity and metrics with application to the Essential Tasks Matrix. Collectively, this qualitative case study will ascertain excess capabilities or shortfalls during the analysis and findings portion of this thesis. The following section outlines the capabilities and type of U.S. military truck companies to signify the magnitude of the IDP issues.

U.S. Military Distribution Capabilities and Considerations

This section delineates the type of U.S. military distribution units and their capabilities to support three million IDPs with nine million meals per day, 2.721 million gallons of bulk potable water per day, 30.06 million gallons of packaged water per day, and 570,000 pounds of medical supplies per day.

Transportation Medium Truck, Cargo Company (40-Ton)

The transportation medium truck cargo company (40-Ton) mission is "to provide transportation for the movement of containerized, non-containerized, palletized, dry and/or refrigerated cargo, and bulk water products."[44] Its capabilities include a total lift capacity of 447 short tons of general cargo and 1,080 pallets.[45] It can also distributed 240,000 gallons of water when equipped with compatible water tank racks.[46] Its major pieces of equipment include 60 M915 trucks and 120 M872 semi-trailers.[47] To appreciate the magnitude of the shortfalls to sustain three million IDPs, the U.S. military will require 142 additional transportation medium truck cargo companies (40-Ton) to use 8,520 M915 trucks and 17,040 M872 semi-trailers.

Quartermaster Water Purification and Distribution Company

The quartermaster water purification and distribution company mission is to "provide direct support water purification, storage, and distribution for brigade and echelons above brigade troops on an area basis."[48] It can distribute 42,000-gallons per day (21,000 per platoon x 2 platoons) using semi-trailer mounted fabric tanks.[49] It can produce 360,000 gallons of potable water per day using a fresh water source.[50] If not using 12 required transportation medium truck cargo companies (40-Ton) to distribute bulk potable water, the U.S. military will require 65 quartermaster water purification and distribution companies to meet the shortfall of 2.721 million gallons per day. The unit can also store up to 160,000 gallons of potable water per day. The storage abilities of 65 quartermaster water purification and distribution companies are sufficient to handle 2.721 million gallons per day. 65 quartermaster water purification and distribution companies can store up to 10,400,000 gallons of water.

Transitution Medium Truck Company (Petroleum,
Oils, Lubricants) (POL) (7,500 gal)

The transportation medium truck company (POL) (7,500 gal) mission is to provide transportation for the movement of bulk petroleum products.[51] With an inventory of 60 7,500-Gallon Semi-Trailers, the company can support a total of 450,000 gallons.[52] Its major pieces of equipment include 60 M915 tractors and 60 7,500-gallon tanker semi-trailers.[53] To support 142 transportation company sized elements across a terrain of roughly 100 miles, the U.S. military requires one Transportation Medium Truck Company (POL) (7,500 gal) to sustain 368,808 gallons per day of fuel in the KTO. Units will have to travel to this company to pick up fuel using supply point distribution. To solve the storage of bulk fuel, one quartermaster petroleum support company can support the bulk fuel storage of up to 5.04 million gallons per day.[54]

Transportation Medium Truck Company
(Palletized Load System)

The transportation medium truck company (PLS) mission is to provide ground transportation for the movement of dry and refrigerated containerized cargo and other general cargo, ammunition, and bottled water on PLS flat-racks.[55] For local haul distribution, where vehicles can make two or more round trips per day based on distance and travel time, a transportation medium truck company (PLS) can transport 1,728 short tons per day.[56] For packaged water to support three million IDPs, the U.S. military requires 103 transportation medium truck companies (PLS) to distribute 122,876 pallets per day.

Sustainment Brigade

A sustainment brigade's mission is to "provide mission command for all subordinate units of the sustainment brigade, synchronize current and future sustainment operations for the expeditionary sustainment command."[57] The sustainment brigade will perform the tactical and operational-level sustainment missions dependent on task organization. The sustainment brigade and combat sustainment support battalions are the higher headquarters for transportation medium truck cargo companies (40-Ton), quartermaster water purification and distribution companies, transportation medium truck companies (POL) (7,500 gal), and transportation medium truck companies (PLS). A sustainment brigade is an organization tailored to its mission. For the KTO, the prospect of two sustainment brigades deploying to sustain operations following North Korean regime collapse is not unlikely.

A sustainment brigade can typically have anywhere from three to seven battalions consisting of ten to twenty companies. However, two sustainment brigades with roughly five transportation companies will decrement the required 142 transportation medium truck cargo companies (40-Ton) to 137. Military sustainment planners instantly can see that the U.S. military, even with deploying two sustainment brigades and five transportation medium truck cargo companies (40-Ton), alone cannot sustain three million IDPs. Even with activating U.S. Army Reserve companies or National Guard

assets, the majority of sustainment will ultimately fall on the ROK.

---

[1]The Huffington Post, "North Korea Skating Close to a Dangerous Line, Says U.S. Defense Secretary Chuck Hagel," April 10, 2013, http://www.huffingtonpost.com/2013/04/10/north-korea-skating-close-dangerous-line-us-defense-secretary-chuck-hagel_n_3054533.html (accessed November 11, 2013).

[2]S. C. M. Paine, *The Sino-Japanese War of 1894-1895: Perceptions, Power, and Primacy* (Cambridge, England: Cambridge University Press, 2005), 316.

[3]Ibid., 321.

[4]Ibid.

[5]Linus Hagström and Marie Soderberg, eds., *North Korea Policy: Japan and the Great Powers* (New York, NY: Routledge, 2006), 57.

[6]Stanley Sandler, *The Korean War: No Victors, No Vanquished* (Lexington, KY: The University Press of Kentucky, 1999), 19-20.

[7]Ibid.

[8]C. Sarah Soh, "Infertility among Korea's "comfort women" survivors: A comparative perspective," *Women's Studies International Forum* 29, no. 1 (January 2006): 67-80, http://dx.doi.org/10.1016/j.wsif.2005.10.007 (accessed April 28, 2014).

[9]Shannon Heit, "Waging sexual warfare: Case studies of rape warfare used by the Japanese Imperial Army during World War II," *Women's Studies International Forum* 32, no. 5 (September 2009): 363-70, http://dx.doi.org/10.1016/j.wsif.2009.07.010 (accessed April 28, 2014).

[10]Michael Wreszin, "The Korean War: A History," *American Communist History* 10, no. 3 (December 2011): 330, http://dx.doi.org/10.1080/14743892.2011.604490 (accessed October 17, 2013).

[11]Jeffrey Grey, "The Korean War," *Journal of Contemporary History* 39, no. 4 (October 2004): 675, http://dx.doi.org/10.1177/0022009404046787 (accessed October 17, 2013).

[12]Hee-Kyung Suh, "Atrocities Before And During The Korean War," *Critical Asian Studies* 42, no. 4 (December 2010): 586, http://dx.doi.org/10.1080/14672715.2010.515388 (accessed October 17, 2013).

[13]Glyn Ford, "North Korea in Transition," *Soundings*, no. 43 (Winter 2009): 126, http://search.proquest.com/docview/211258761?accountid=458.

[14]Hyun Sik Kim, "The Secret History of Kim Jong Il, *Foreign Policy*, no. 168 (September 2008): 443, http://search.proquest.com/docview/224037546?accountid=458.

[15]Samuel S. Kim and Tai Hwan Lee, *North Korea and Northeast Asia* (Lanham, MD: Rowman and Littlefield Publishers, 2002), 124.

[16]Jae-Cheon Lim "North Korea's Hereditary Succession," *Asian Survey* 52, no. 3 (June 2012): 553, http://dx.doi.org/10.1525/as.2012.52.3.550 (accessed October 17, 2013).

[17]Han S. Park, ed., *North Korea: Ideology, Politics, Economy* (Englewood Cliffs, NJ: Prentice Hall College Div, 1996), 53.

[18]Mitchell Lerner, "'Mostly Propaganda in Nature': Kim Il Sung, the Juche Ideology, and the Second Korean War," *Woodrow Wilson International Center for Scholars: North Korea International Documentation Project* 1, no. 3 (December 2010): 1-102.

[19]Suh, "Atrocities Before And During The Korean War," 554.

[20]Bruce W. Bennett, *Uncertainties in the North Korean Nuclear Threat* (Santa Monica, CA: Rand, 2010), vii.

[21]Ibid.

[22]Kim and Lee, *North Korea and Northeast Asia*, 53.

[23]Mark Fitzpatrick "Stopping Nuclear North Korea," *Survival* 51, no. 4 (September 2009): 9, http://dx.doi.org/10.1080/00396330903168782 (accessed October 17, 2013).

[24]Ibid., 12.

[25]Ford. "North Korea in Transition," 134.

[26]Lim "North Korea's Hereditary Succession," 565.

[27]Kim and Lee, *North Korea and Northeast Asia*, 182.

[28]U.S. Joint Chiefs of Staff, Joint Publication 4-0, *Joint Logistics* (Washington, DC: U.S. Joint Chiefs of Staff, October 16, 2013), I-1.

[29]Kim and Lee, *North Korea and Northeast Asia*, 52.

[30]Bennett, *Uncertainties in the North Korean Nuclear Threat*, viii.

[31]Ibid.

[32]Ibid., x.

[33]Headquarters, Army Forces Far East, *Logistics Study of the Korean Campaigns: 1950-1953* (San Francisco, CA: Operations Research Office), 5.

[34]T R. Fehrenbach, *This Kind of War: The Classic Korean War History*, 50th ed (Washington, DC: Brassey, 2000), 314.

[35]Headquarters, Army Forces Far East, *Logistics Study of the Korean Campaigns*, 5.

[36]Steve Waddell, *United States Army Logistics: From the American Revolution to 9/11* (Santa Barbara: Greenwood Publishing Group, 2010), 155.

[37]Thomas Herren. Briefing Conference on the Republic of Korea for Unified Command Mission to the ROK (Tokyo, General Headquarters, United Nations Command, 1952).

[38]Headquarters, Army Forces Far East, *Logistics Study of the Korean Campaigns*, 6.

[39]Michael Cyril, *Operational Logistics* (Fort Leavenworth, KS: United States Army Command and General Staff College, 2001), 2.

[40]John R. Tibbetts, *Power Projection Logistics: What Theater Support Unit?* (Fort Leavenworth, KS: United States Army Command and General Staff College, 1995), 17.

[41]Steven Pate, *Transforming Logistics: Joint Theater Logistics* (Carlisle, PA: U.S. Army War College, 2006), 18.

[42]Charles R. Shrader, *Communist Logistics in the Korean War* (Westport, CT: Greenwood Press, 1995), 18.

[43]Central Intelligence Agency, "The World Factbook: North Korea," CIA World Factbook, https://www.cia.gov/library/publications/the-world-factbook/geos/kn.html (accessed May 1, 2014).

[44]U.S. Army Command and General Staff College, Student Text 4-1, *Theater Sustainment Battle Book* (Fort Leavenworth, KS: U.S. Army Command and General Staff College, June 2013), 6-34.

[45]Ibid.

[46]Ibid.

[47]Ibid.

[48]Ibid., 6-32.

[49]Ibid.

[50]Ibid.

[51]Ibid., 6-36.

[52]Ibid.

[53]Ibid.

[54]Ibid., 6-29.

[55]Ibid., 6-37.

[56]Ibid.

[57]Ibid., 5-10.

CHAPTER 3

RESEARCH METHODOLOGY

This chapter outlines the research design and methodology of this study. This study uses a qualitative research methodology and uses a case study research design. This section will contain research methodology, sources of data, and sampling of case studies. This manuscript adopts a qualitative research approach, as "the use of rigorous qualitative research methods can enhance the development of quality measures, the development and dissemination of comparative quality reports, as well as quality improvement efforts."[1] This study enables the target audience to adopt an enhanced view of the sustainment architecture on the Korean peninsula. This thesis also examines how current U.S. military assets successfully support a regime collapse and its shortfalls. These case studies provide a framework of the study through the sustainment perspective.

Qualitative Case Study Research Design

According to Dr. Robert K. Yin, the case study is "best when a need exists to study a critical case, an extreme or unique case, or a revelatory case."[2] The study of sustainment implications and ramifications of the North Korean regime collapse contains limited access to the body of research. Most of the research intelligence and data derives from recently unclassified military documents and political manuscripts that add validity and credibility to the review. This study will exercise a holistic design with embedded vignettes.

As discussed in the aforementioned sections, the assumptions outlining a North Korean regime collapse include a dynamic combined arms environment with a humanitarian aid effort. Because of these assumptions, qualitative case study research employs an "in-depth description and analysis of a bounded system."[3] Furthermore, "case study research is [a] qualitative approach in which the investigator explores a bounded system or multiple bounded systems over time, through detailed, in-depth data collection involving multiple sources of information."[4] This manuscript will analyze data based on assumptions, assess trends and the current sustainment posture, and make a recommendation for the use of United States sustainment forces.

Sources of Data

The study uses three separate historical case studies of Yugoslavia, Ethiopia, and the Haiti earthquake humanitarian relief efforts in an effort to satisfy the aforementioned assumptions of a North Korean regime collapse. The first set of literature outlines post-conflict resolution in Yugoslavia. The Yugoslavian case study serves to reflect on a relatively successful post-conflict resolution. The second set of literature provides the example of Ethiopia with particular regard to Eritrea and its lessons learned. The Ethiopian case study serves to highlight a historical case study that reflects a relatively unsuccessful attempt at post-conflict resolution. The final set of literature outlines resolution of internally displaced persons in a disastrous environment using Haiti relief efforts as an operational model.

The author will determine how the U.S. military in conjunction with allied nations' militaries can meet the goals established to support the North Korean regime collapse suitably, acceptably, and feasibly. By comparing the historical case studies, the author will determine what changes are necessary that meet the criteria for sustainable conflict on the Korean peninsula. Finally, the author will examine published research documents by military and civilian researchers that address post-conflict reconstruction and apply it to the fundamental assets in the U.S. military sustainment inventory and operational strategies. In order to answer the primary research question, the author must use subjective and interpretive analysis. In this case, interpretive and critical perspectives overlap.

Purposeful Sampling

Purposeful sampling methods serve to adopt primary research reports on a related topic. "The logic and power of purposeful sampling in selecting information-rich cases for study in depth."[5] Because of North Korean regime collapse, the historical vignettes of Yugoslavia, Ethiopia, and Haiti serve as information-rich cases that are relevant in this qualitative case study.

Purposeful sampling methods involve "purposeful selection, review, analysis and synthesis of primary research reports on a similar topic . . . readers [possess] sufficient information . . . so that they can make informed decisions . . . to their own contexts."[6] A combination approach to purposeful sampling procedures uses criterion sampling and typical case sampling. The logic of criterion sampling is to peruse, review, and study all cases that meet some predetermined criterion of importance to achieve commonality.[7] Because of the complex and ambiguous nature of the problem depicted in the thesis assertion, this thesis includes qualitative methods as "describing a culture or program to people not familiar with the setting studied . . . can [prove] helpful to provide a qualitative profile of one or more typical cases."[8]

Typical case sampling involves "selecting those cases that are the most typical, normal, or representative of the group of cases under consideration."[9] Applying case

53

study analysis and purposeful sampling procedures, Yugoslavia relates to North Korea because of its related collapse during the post-Tito years and the Balkan crises; a North Korean regime collapse would have similar repercussions to sustainment.

Yugoslavia serves as a relatively successful post-conflict reconstruction effort by NATO. An Ethiopian study serves as a source where a post-conflict resolution was not adequate and identifies shortfalls. These shortfalls or restraints will aid the process of identifying how the U.S. military can sustain a North Korean regime collapse. Haiti's earthquake incorporates the sustainment of internally displaced persons and refugees synonymous with a North Korea regime collapse.

Data Triangulation

Practitioners use data triangulation with a wide variety of data sources to provide a holistic picture, as no single measure of research can adequately solve the problem of "rival causal factors . . . multiple methods of observations must be employed."[10] There is a lack of common terms, coding, and measurable yardsticks in post-conflict reconstruction in U.S. government literature and independent research services such as the Research and Development (RAND) Corporation.

In qualitative research, "triangulation strengthens a study by combining methods."[11] Furthermore, "triangulation serves to assess [the] reader's consistency in qualitative coding across texts that he or she coded, with themes and categories serving as yardsticks."[12] To determine qualitative measures of post-conflict resolution in the historical case studies, the applied analysis model in this manuscript is the U.S. Department of State Post-Conflict Reconstruction Essential Tasks Matrix (ETM). This matrix serves as a checklist, or qualitative yardstick for post-conflict reconstruction.

The Department of State Post-Conflict Reconstruction Essential Tasks Matrix

The essential tasks matrix separates into five technical sectors (security, governance and participation, humanitarian assistance and social well-being, economic stabilization and infrastructure, and justice and reconciliation).[13]

ETM: Technical Sectors

Of the five technical sectors, therein lies a significant host of 1,178 individual tasks that cross-pollinate and crosscut to force planners to reference other sectors. This thesis includes examination of the five technical sectors.

Security

Security is the first of five technical sectors in the ETM. Within the security construct, seven sub-constructs exist. The first one is disposition of armed forces, intelligence services, and belligerents that emphasize cessation of hostilities, enforcement of peace agreements, disposition and constitution of national armed services, disarmament, demobilization, reintegration of combatants, and disposition of national intelligence services. Security is the sector organic to a U.S. military sustainment planner's objectives. The military sustainment planner considers logistics of the armed forces, IDPs, and other commodities required to sustain momentum.

Governance and Participation

Governance and participation is the second of five major sections in the essential tasks matrix. Governance concentrates on national constituting processes, transitional governance, executive authority, legislative strengthening, local governance, transparency, and anti-corruption. Participation focuses on elections, political parties, civil society, media, and public information. The sustainment planner considers required supplies to achieve strategic victory through local elections and legislative strengthening. He or she may have to procure construction supplies or office supplies to facilitate the legitimacy of a newly established government.

Humanitarian Assistance and Social Well-Being

Humanitarian and social well-being is the third section and has the most detail out of the five technical sectors. Within this construct, several sub-constructs exist. Of most importance are refugees and internally displaced persons that emphasize prevention of population displacements, refugee assistance, internally displaced persons support, and camp security. Next, food security illustrates famine prevention, emergency food relief, and food market response.

Sustainment planners incorporate subsistence planning to ensure no looting of field rations. Shelter and non-food relief that highlight non-food relief distribution and shelter construction may require the sustainment planner to consider agreements with non-governmental organizations. Medical planners consider potable water management, waste management, medical capacity, public health clinics, hospital facilities, human resources development for health care, health policy, health funding, prevention of epidemics, nutrition, reproductive health, environmental health, and community health education. Human resources managers plans for personnel services and apply skill sets on the development of fundamental schools, universities, literacy campaigns, and core curriculum planning.

Economic Stabilization and Infrastructure

Economic stabilization and infrastructure is the fourth major part in the matrix. Economic stabilization concentrates on employment generation, fiscal policy and governance, economic policy, trading of imports and exports, market economics, and the social safety net. The sustainment planner considers economic impacts to the flow of supplies coming into the ports or airfields. Sustainment planners have to plan and anticipate construction or barrier materiel to build up infrastructure such as municipal services through coordination with other services. Others methods are engineering support and contracting support.

Justice and Reconciliation

Justice and reconciliation is the fifth and final major part. The sub-constructs are the interim criminal justice system, indigenous police, judicial personnel and infrastructure, adjudication of property, legal system reform, human rights standards, corrections, war crime courts, truth commissions and remembrance, and community rebuilding. The sustainment planner considers supporting justice and reconciliation by planning for the subsistence of any prisoners of war to abide by international law.

Validity of Design

The matrix encourages cross sectoring conducting a comprehensive analysis, but purposefully (by design) avoids any dialectical or counterproductive cross-referencing that would otherwise become a cumbersome planning tool.[14] The interrelationships are the key to this design, as planners likely will find that one technical sector dovetails naturally to other technical sectors or individual tasks. The linkages intrinsically are dyads that lead to triads as any subsequent analysis can provide fruitful, interesting, enlightening, elegant, and sophisticated conclusions or arguments.

The ETM serves as a document catalog of the results of interagency working group discussions led by the State Department's Office of the Coordinator for Reconstruction and Stabilization. Because the Department of Defense does not have a reconstruction matrix to gauge sustainment requirements in a post-conflict reconstruction effort, this tool from the State Department plans to support countries in transition from conflict of civil strife.[15] This thesis uses this matrix because of its applicability in North Korea as a post-conflict reconstruction scenario. The ETM will likely not gain the unanimity regarding the assignment of all tasks into respective expectations.

One may argue the validity of an ETM tool because it lacks the mathematics involved regarding short tons or gallons. However, too often in U.S. military history, the inability or lack of U.S. military sustainment planners to forecast and anticipate requirements in advance denies the extension of operational reach or maximizing momentum to advance U.S. strategic interests. The ETM provides a different type of analysis that forces military sustainment planners to analyze scenarios traditionally that are initially not priorities. Numerous practitioners employed the ETM in studies and research papers. Researchers discovered the ETM as part of the book *Winning the Peace: An American Strategy for Post-Conflict Reconstruction* as it also influenced the U.S. Army's Field Manual 3-07 (*Stability Operations*).[16]

The ETM is a tool that can help identify gaps in capabilities, especially sustainment capabilities, to ensure that the required capabilities are either developed within the U.S. government or sought out.[17] "The value of the matrix is inculcating a common language that captures stability, security, transition, and reconstruction operations. The ETM developed from an earlier compilation put together by the Center for Strategic and International Studies and the Association of the United States Army revised in Interagency Working Groups.[18] Combatant commands and joint forces command widely used the ETM during Operation Iraqi Freedom and Operation Enduring Freedom, particularly the Joint Interagency Coordination Group (a staff proponent responsible for interagency affairs).[19]

The RAND study, *Preparing the Army for Stability Operations: Doctrinal and Interagency Issues*, used the ETM in application to the deployments to the U.S.-Mexico border, Operation Enduring Freedom, Operation Iraqi Freedom, and Army operations in the Balkans. The ETM was a tool used by the Atlantic Council of the United States' program on international security to study NATO and its stabilization operations.[20]

Researchers acknowledged the function of the ETM in the Post-Conflict Resolution Project sanctioned by the Center for Strategic and International Studies in measuring Iraq's reconstruction.[21] As part of the U.S. Presidential mandate for active planning implementation, based on National Security Presidential Directive 44, throughout all the geographic combatant commands in 2005, U.S. European Command inculcated the ETM in the Strategy, Plans and Assessments Directorate to evaluate their theater security cooperation strategy.[22] The ETM also influenced research at the Colonel Arthur D. Simons Center for the study of interagency cooperation at Fort Leavenworth, Kansas through inquiries of Iraq and Afghanistan and the State Department Coordinator for reconstruction and stabilization.[23] Outlined below in a table are the goals of the ETM's 1,178 individual tasks functionally and temporally organized.

Table 4.   ETM Goals (Five Technical Sectors in Three Phases)

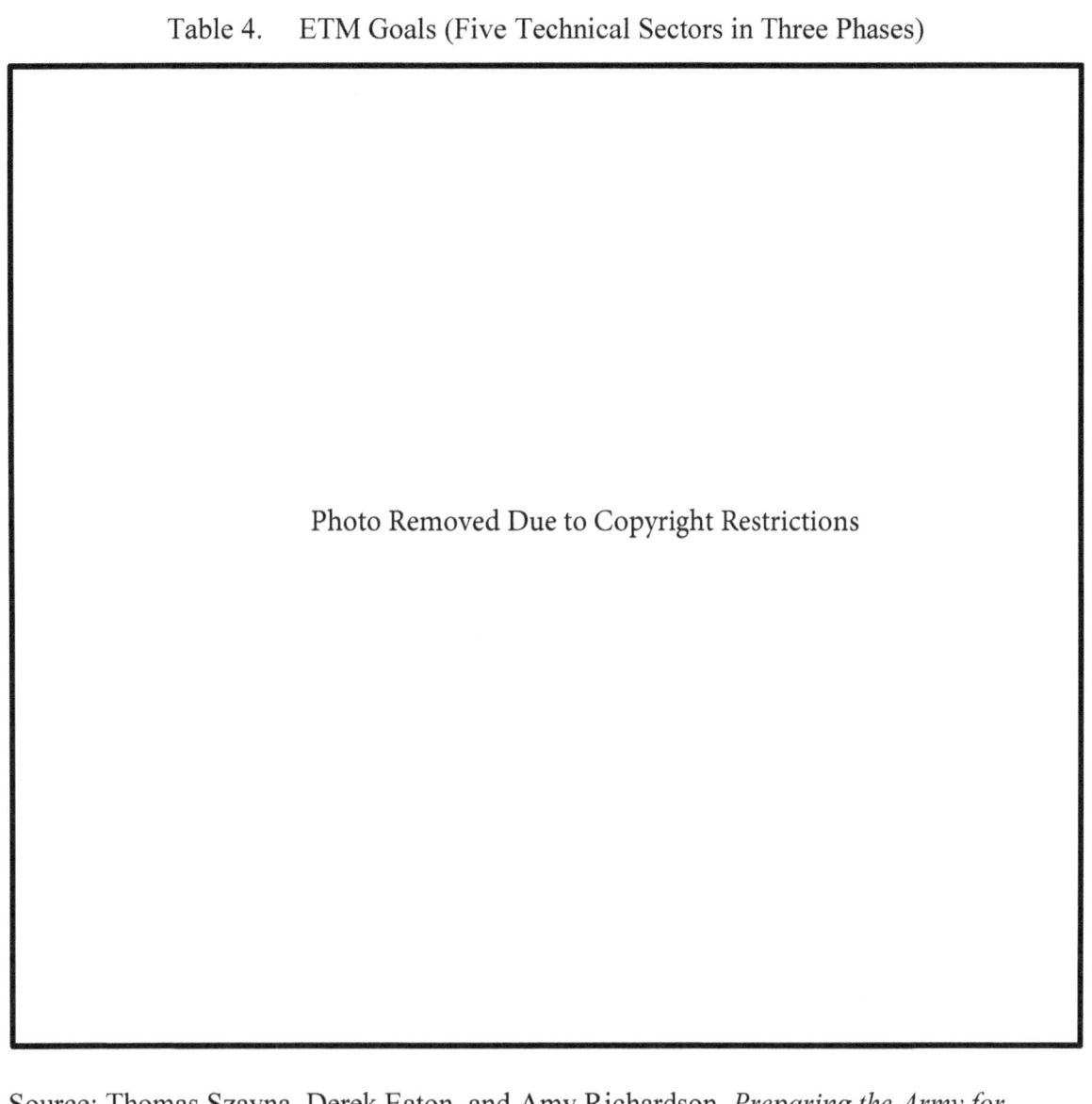

Photo Removed Due to Copyright Restrictions

Source: Thomas Szayna, Derek Eaton, and Amy Richardson, *Preparing the Army for Stability Operations: Doctrinal and Interagency Issues* (Santa Monica, CA: Rand, 2007), 17.

This matrix has the necessary components and sequencing of tasks to appraise sustainment architecture on the KTO. Cross-pollination of tasks is not a new concept, especially when using interdepartmental products to appreciate the thoroughness of applied assessments.

The Three Phases of the ETM (Short, Mid, and Long Term)

The ETM is organization by analyzing each technical sector in three conceptual phases of time and space: actions in (1) a recommended initial response (short-term), (2) actions during a transformation period (mid-term), and (3) actions to foster sustainability (long-term). For example, using the security technical sector, the initial response phase in regime collapse is to establish a safe environment. Actions during the transformation period phase are developing legitimate and stable security institutions and organizations. The recommended action during the fostering sustainability phase is incorporating indigenous capacity.

The ETM incorporates all the instruments of power with a whole-of-government approach. The ETM positions the sustainment planner to widen his or her aperture beyond the sustainment of CFC and USFK with fuel, bullets, bandages, and water. Through application of the ETM, the sustainment planner can infer and anticipate other sustainment missions by observing the ETM technical sectors other than security. Examples of other sustainment missions include, but are not limited to sustaining local elections, internment and resettlement activities, detainee operations, contracting operations, multinational logistics, humanitarian aid packages, effects of global economic imports and exports at ports of embarkation on U.S. military supplies, and building local infrastructure.

Figure 8. Sample Screenshots of the Essential Tasks Matrix

Source: United States Department of State, *Post-Conflict Reconstruction Essential Tasks* (Washington, DC: U.S. Government Printing Office, April 2005), http://pksoi.army.mil/ doctrine_concepts/documents/SCRC%20and%20J7/SCRS%20PCR%20Essential%20Tas ks%205%201%202005.pdf (accessed April 29, 2014).

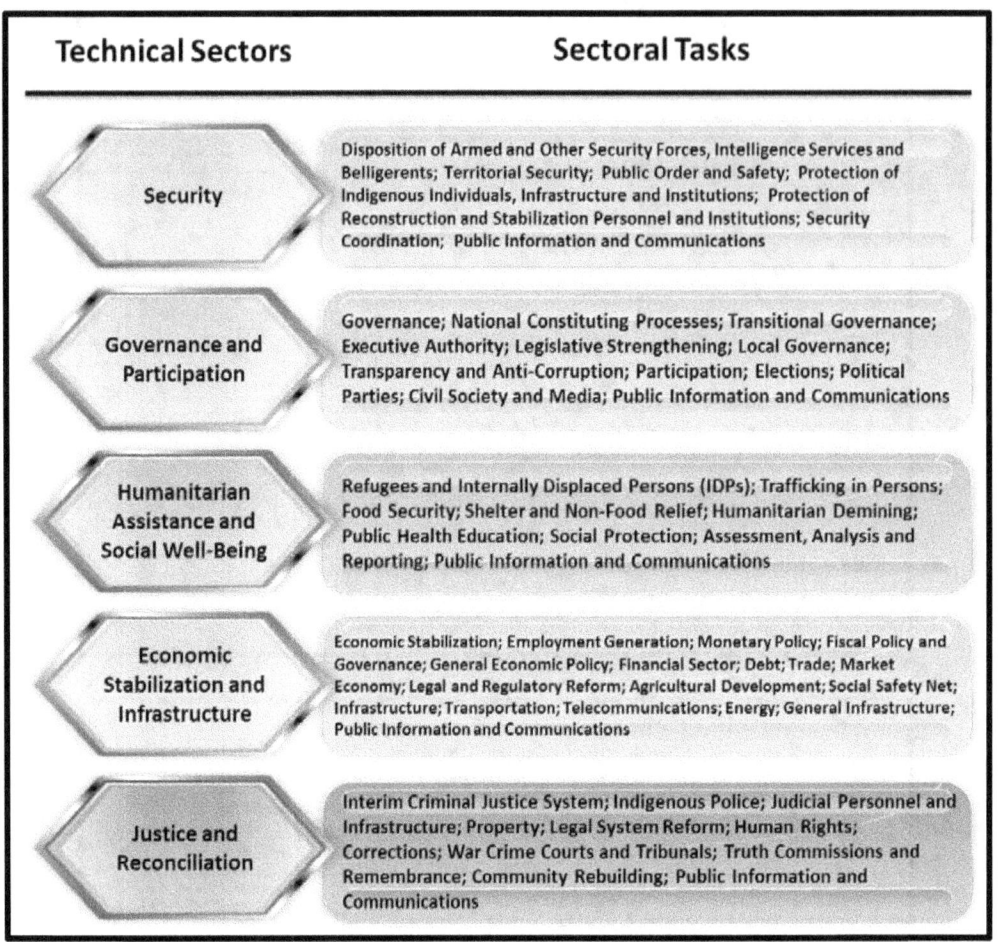

Figure 8. State Department Reconstruction and Stabilization Essential Tasks Matrix

Source: Figure graphics created by author. Content derived from Office of the Coordinator for Reconstruction and Stabilization, United States Department of State, *Post-Conflict Reconstruction Essential Tasks* (Washington, DC: U.S. Government Printing Office, April 2005).

Case Study: Yugoslavia

These major themes contain detailed and intricate qualitative parameters that allow the reader to justify significant assessments of Yugoslavia, Ethiopia, and Haiti against the Korean peninsula. Some of the general lessons that stand out in Yugoslavia include the limited role of outside military force in resolving ethnic conflict and the importance of economic advantage.[24] The Yugoslavian case study will emanate lessons learned for planners to apply to North Korean regime collapse using outside military forces and economic advantages. Early intervention is also an imperative condition that will contribute to the progression in this body of research.

Case Study: Ethiopia

The aftermath of Ethiopia's conflict is the secondary case study, specifically the case of Eritrean independence. Scholars viewed Eritrea as a beacon of hope for a new Africa but over two decades later, Esayas Afeworki turned hope into anguish by misusing [the] trust and betraying confidence.[25] Eritrea suffered thirty years of armed struggle with against an Ethiopian state where Eritrea's quest for legitimacy aggravated the United Nation's quest for a stable region and its misshaped destiny.[26] The Horn of Africa contains relevant analyses when comparing conflict resolution on the Korean peninsula as the situation implies sovereignty and territorial integrity, borders, independence and self-determination, and nation-building.[27]

Case Study: Haiti

The Haiti earthquake case study serves as an example for channeling internally displaced persons as the earthquake "killed more than 316,000 people, injured 300,000 others, and displaced more than 1 million people."[28] The Haiti catastrophic natural disaster is not a regime collapse, but its response structure can teach some lessons for the Korean peninsula.

Synthesis of Case Studies to North Korea

These three case studies, through purposeful sampling and data triangulation,

capture the elements of a dynamic nature of North Korean regime collapse. Their

applications to post-conflict reconstruction efforts can provide useful expectations and

gap analysis to indicate any demand signals that are not getting enough attention.

Coupled with the numbers given in the sustainment architecture, the qualitative case

study can also reflect some improvements by priority and any shortfalls in other areas.

---

[1]Shoshanna Sofaer, "Qualitative Research Methods," *International Journal for Quality in Health Care* 14, no. 4 (August 2002): 329, http://dx.doi.org/10.1093/intqhc/14.4.329 (accessed January 28, 2014).

[2]John W. Creswell, *Qualitative Inquiry and Research Design: Choosing Among Five Approaches*, 3rd ed (Thousand Oaks: SAGE, 2012), 196.

[3]Sharan B. Merriam, *Qualitative Research: a Guide to Design and Implementation*, 3rd ed. (San Francisco: Jossey-Bass, 2009), 43.

[4]Ibid.

[5]Michael Quinn Patton, *Qualitative Research and Evaluation Methods*, 3rd ed (Thousand Oaks, CA: SAGE Publications, Inc, 2002), 230.

[6]Harsh Suri, "Purposeful Sampling in Qualitative Research Synthesis," *Qualitative Research Journal* 11, no. 2 (2011): 63-75, http://dx.doi.org/10.3316/QRJ1102063 (accessed January 28, 2014).

[7]Patton, *Qualitative Research and Evaluation Methods*, 238.

[8]Ibid., 236.

[9]Charles Teddlie and Abbas Tashakkori, *Foundations of Mixed Methods Research: Integrating Quantitative and Qualitative Approaches in the Social and Behavioral Sciences* (Los Angeles: SAGE, 2009), 176.

[10]Ibid.

[11]Patton, *Qualitative Research and Evaluation Methods*, 247.

[12]Anton Oleinik, "Mixing quantitative and qualitative content analysis: Triangulation at work," *Quality and Quantity* 45, no. 4: 859-873, http://dx.doi.org/ 10.1007/s11135-010-9399-4 (accessed January 28, 2014).

[13]John R. Schmidt, "Can Outsiders Bring Democracy to Post-Conflict States?," *Orbis* 52, no. 1 (January 2008): 107-22, http://dx.doi.org/10.1016/ j.orbis.2007.10.008 (accessed April 28, 2014).

[14]Nora Bensahel, "Organising for Nation Building," *Survival* 49, no. 2 (June 2007): 43-76, http://dx.doi.org/10.1080/00396330701437827 (accessed April 28, 2014).

[15]Sarah Beller, Graig Klein, and Ronald Fisher, *US Government Innovations in Peacebuilding and Conflict Resolution: Implications for the IPCR Program* (Washington, DC: School of International Service (SIS), American University, 2010), 29.

[16]Shon McCormick, "A Primer On Developing Measures of Effectiveness," *Military Review* 90, no. 4 (July-August 2010): 60.

[17]Thomas Szayna, Derek Eaton, and Amy Richardson, *Preparing the Army for Stability Operations: Doctrinal and Interagency Issues* (Santa Monica, CA: Rand, 2007), 16.

[18]Ibid.

[19]Ibid.

[20]Richard Nelson, *How Should NATO Handle Stabilization Operations and Reconstruction Efforts?* (Washington, DC: Atlantic Council of the United States: Program on International Security, 2006), I-1.

[21]Frederick Barton and Bathsheba Crocker, *Progress or Peril? Measuring Iraq's Reconstruction: The Post-Conflict Reconstruction Project* (Washington, DC: Center for Strategic and International Studies, 2004), 1.

[22]Michael Pryce, *Improving S/CRS Planning Framework from a Geographic Combatant Command's Perspective: Analysis for Civil-Military Transitions* (Boiling Springs, PA: The Cornwallis Group XI, 2005), 175.

[23]Jay Liddick and David Anderson, "State Department/Coordinator for Reconstruction and Stabilization: Inception, Challenges, and Impact on U.S. Reconstruction and Stabilization Capacity," *Interagency Paper* 4, no. 1 (April 2011): 10.

[24]James B. Steinberg and Ford Foundation, *The Role of European Institutions in Security after the Cold War: Some Lessons from Yugoslavia* (Santa Monica, CA: Rand, 1992), vi.

[25]Siegfried Pausewang, "Eritrea: A Dream Deferred," *Forum for Development Studies* 37, no. 3 (November 2010): 415-16, http://dx.doi.org/10.1080/08039410.2010.512416 (accessed January 28, 2014).

[26]Ruth Iyob, *The Eritrean Struggle for Independence: Domination, Resistance, Nationalism, 1941-1993 (African Studies)* (Cambridge: Cambridge University Press, 1997), 133.

[27]Leenco Lata, "The Ethiopia-Eritrea War," *Review of African Political Economy* 30, no. 97 (2003): 379.

[28]Gary Cecchine, Forrest E. Morgan, Michael A. Wermuth, Timothy Jackson, Agnes Gereben Schaefer, and Matthew Stafford, *The U.S. Military Response to the 2010 Haiti Earthquake: Considerations for Army Leaders* (Santa Monica, CA: Rand, 2013), 115.

CHAPTER 4

ANALYSIS

Introduction

During this analysis, Yugoslavia, Bosnia-Herzegovina, and Haiti are the case studies with application to and discussion of the ETM's five technical sectors. Beyond the ETM, a paragraph of U.S. military sustainment outlines sustainment actions from the joint force for that particular case study. After the three case study's ETM analysis and sustainment discussion, each relates to North Korea implications. A table at the end of this chapter presents the summary of findings.

Case Study I Yugoslavia: Background

Marshall Tito led Yugoslavia, declared it the Socialist Federal Republic of Yugoslavia and became its perennial leader after the Second World War.[1] Under Tito's rule, Yugoslavia consisted of six republics: Serbia, Croatia, Montenegro, Slovenia, Bosnia, and Macedonia. Tito was the only leader able to make these hostile persons in each of the six republics act civilly towards one another.[2] After Tito's death in 1980, nationalism between republics rose.[3]

After forty years of relative peaceful conditions, a former bank president by the name of Slobodan Milosevic became President of Serbia while stirring up ethnic tensions and dividing the republics.[4] By March 1989, the Serbian Assembly abolished Tito's political autonomy to the two provinces of Vojvodina and Kosovo.[5] By 1989, Milosevic controlled Yugoslavia through the dominance of Serbia. This marked the beginning of Yugoslavia's disintegration.

Security

In the former Yugoslavia from 1992 to 1995, the United Nations established United Nations Protected Areas (UNPAs) in the organization of effective sanctuaries during protracted conflicts.[6] Under United Nations (UN) Security Council Resolution 743 in February 1992, during the Croatian War of Independence and the Yugoslav Wars, the United Nations Protection Force (UNPROFOR) conducted security in demilitarized enclaves.

Phase I: Initial Response

Outsiders included governments or international organizations. UNPROFOR established UNPAs in Croatia in February 1992 that followed the January 2 cease-fire between Croat and Serb forces brokered by the UN secretary-general's special representative.[7] The UN created three UNPAs in Eastern Slavonia, Western Slavonia, and Krajina in order to disarm, demobilize, and disband all irregular forces.[8] Furthermore, UN-supplied civilian police assisted the local law enforcement to ensure basic human rights enforcement within the zones.[9]

Phase II: Transformation

The UNPROFOR's mission ensured the delivery of relief supplies to local inhabitants. This mission was coterminous with the Fall 1992/Spring 1993 efforts of the Bosnian Serbs "to drive all Muslims out of the Drina Valley . . . to [eliminate] all such communities from Eastern Bosnia."[10] As a result of this conflict, the UN Security Council declared Srebrenica a safe area and "authorized the dispatch of seventy-six hundred troops" and air power capabilities.[11]

Over time, NATO established an exclusion zone to besiege aggressive Serbs. The UN Security Council established a resolution prohibiting flights in Bosnia air space in October 1992. A UN contingent of roughly 200 staff officers established operations in Bosnia in spring 1992, as their initial mission was to establish the UN headquarters for peace operations in Croatia.[12] In March 1993, the UN Security Council passed Resolution 836, which created safe areas around Muslim towns that were resisting the Serbs.[13]

Phase III: Fostering Sustainability

In the weeks after the Dayton Peace Agreement in December 1995, 20,000 U.S. soldiers deployed to Bosnia and a massive international reconstruction effort began. Ten years later, the United States and its European allies remained a presence in the region.[14] By executing stability and sustainment operations, NATO showed it could embrace the role of a peace maker; by taking on the commitment to establish peace agreements with 60,000 troops, NATO was a peace enforcer.[15]

Governance and Participation

Power politics drove most of the conflicts in Bosnia by elites who manipulated deeply rooted ethnic tensions to benefit their quests for political and economic supremacy.[16] Global superpowers viewed Yugoslavia as an opportunity to promote specific agendas that led to proxy wars.

Phase I: Initial Response

Under President George H.W. Bush's administration, media outrage and public disgust in the wake concentration camps in Omarska, Temelin, and other central Bosnian towns prompted action, but nothing happened until the UN became involved."[17] Finally,

70

in December 1992 the Bush administration attempted to persuade the Europeans to support lifting the international arms embargo on Bosnia in an effort to placate regional instability but did not positively eliminate strife and dissension.[18] When Bush left office in 1992, President William Clinton's administration preferred to avoid unilateral action, accepting Secretary of State Warren Christopher's emphasis that the situation in Serbia was entirely a European problem.

Photo Removed Due to Copyright Restrictions

Figure 9. The Balkan States of the former Yugoslavia

Source: The University of North Carolina-Chapel Hill, "What Happened to Yugoslavia? the War, the Peace and the Future: Examining NATO and the Evolution of the Trans-Atlantic Relationship," *Center for European Studies UNC– Chapel Hill* (Fall 2004): 1-16.

Phase II: Transformation

The Serbs came to negotiation talks in 1995 when force coupled with diplomatic efforts.[19] The Dayton Peace Accords stipulated that Bosnia was to remain sovereign in name, with two contiguous territories—one for the Serbs and the other for the Muslims and Croats and a weak central government.[20] The U.S. entered the situation in 1994 and took an active role in resolving the conflict, finally ending it in 1995.[21] Other than the U.S., Britain, France, Germany, or effectively, key European NATO members collectively agonized over the fate of Bosnia.[22]

Phase III: Fostering Sustainability

Anticipating the potential for European instability being uncertain of the Balkan crisis, "the United States quickly fell in line with the European proposal to establish safe areas for endangered Muslim towns and Sarajevo, which was manifested in the UN Security Council Resolution 836."[23] The Clinton Administration made every effort to nest their policies with those of European allies.

Humanitarian Assistance and Social Well-Being

In regards to refugee assistance, the European nations tended to be more pragmatic as their immediate concerns involved stemming the refugee flow. European leadership sought to repatriate those who had sought protection or assistance in their countries. From the outset, European leadership wanted to contain the conflict, which was also a primary goal of the U.S.[24]

Phase I: Initial Response

Yugoslavia found itself in a situation of ethnic cleansing. The struggle with United Nations High Commissioner for Refugees (UNHCR) was to avoid the perception of creating refugees when carrying out substantial evacuations of affected people."[25] Information operations for the UN and U.S. armed forces were keys to shaping the perception to reflect Bosnian sovereignty on the world stage. The alternative action was to try and provide security to threatened minorities where they lived, but proved to be an unrealistic option in a situation of ethnic cleansing.[26] One lesson learned from this situation was that policy makers should define early the definition of UNHCR's protection policy for refugees toward facilitating departure from violence and life-threatening circumstances.

Phase II: Transformation

Media played a positive role in displaying U.S. airdrops of aid, emergency medical evacuations from Sarajevo by the United Kingdom, and NATO's protection measures for the Bosnian capital."[27] In hindsight, because of the lack of early-established policy, the actions appeared to be exercises in damage control in response to intergovernmental incompetence.[28] In retrospect, a clearly defined protection policy from the outset establishes predictability for sustainment planners to forecast sufficient consumption rates and construction material.

Phase III: Fostering Sustainability

Unique circumstances in the Yugoslavian area drove many humanitarian organizations, political organizations, and military organizations beyond traditional missions and standard operating procedures. These circumstances tested the limits of both expertise and comparative advantage.[29] Furthermore, because of the heightened security situation among the Serbian attacks, the UNHCR used bulletproof vests and armored vehicles for the first time in a major operation."[30] NATO launched air strikes against Yugoslavian military targets that lasted for 78 days. Concurrently, in Kosovo, thousands fled attacks by Serb forces with a mass exodus into Albania and Macedonia, where NATO and other troops provided emergency aid.[31] In Yugoslavia, not unlike the North Korean situation proposed in this thesis, an environment with both an armed conflict with a mass exodus of refugees interplay with the sustainability efforts of the U.S. military and other nations' contributions.

Economic Stabilization and Infrastructure

New international conditions inundated the ill-prepared Yugoslav state with complexities. The dire economic and political state of affairs within the federation compounded such intricacies and generated divisive and heated debates on the future of the state.[32]

Phase I: Initial Response

The Kosovo war impacted six regional economies with an average decline in growth of one percent, coupled with a decline in output of about two percentage points"[33] By June 1994, the UN team threatened the Serbs with lifting the arms embargo from the Federation if they refused to sign. Concurrently, the team promised to lift the economic embargo on Serbia–Montenegro if they did sign. The Serbs rejected the plan and in response, increased sniping and shelling in Sarajevo.[34]

Phase II: Transformation

Bulgaria was a nation that suffered reduced exports and foreign investment that led to a slowdown in growth by two and a half percentage points.[35] For Romania, the worst economic effect happened as NATO warplanes targeted bridges over the Danube, blocking both sea transports along the river and rail traffic across it during the 1999 NATO air war with Serbia. Lost trade and higher transportation expenses cost Bucharest $30 million to $50 million per week.[36] Macedonia did not experience a full-blown war, but the conflict deprived Macedonia of exports that led to high unemployment rates."[37] Other countries that suffered from the Kosovo conflict included Austria, Hungary, Italy, Greece, Ukraine, and even Moldova from loss of tourism, loss of trade, and refugees.[38]

Phase III: Fostering Sustainability

In May 1995, the United States initiated talks with Milosevic despite divisions within the U.S. government. In exchange for Yugoslavian or Serbian recognition of Bosnia, leaders would remove the economic embargo.[39] Because of the economic impacts of war, the UN and U.S. participated in economic recovery plans throughout the region. In application to North Korea, neighboring territories may experience similar decrements in economic considerations. A flourishing global economy enabled the Western nations to leverage their economic power, assisting Yugoslavia in consolidating its buffer role between the two blocs of the Cold War system.[40] NATO interventions in Yugoslavia were successful because of the mitigation of economic costs inflicted on states neighboring the former Yugoslavia. Most adjacent territories suffered damage as mentioned, but in no instance was it catastrophic.[41]

Justice and Reconciliation

The UN established the International Criminal Tribunal for the former Yugoslavia (ICTY) in 1993 by the UN Security Council Resolution 827. As of September 2011 the ICTY indicted 161 persons.[42]

Phase I: Initial Response

The ICTY indictments addressed crimes committed between 1991 and 2001 the former six republics of Yugoslavia. The legal landmarks included the creation of war crimes tribunals to deal with violations of international humanitarian law in the former Yugoslavia and international criminal court with universal jurisdiction over crimes against humanity.[43] In the first genocide conviction, the ICTY found former general Radislav Krstic guilty in July 1995, and they sentenced him to 46 years in prison for the massacre of Muslim men and boys from Srebrenica.[44]

Phase II: Transformation

Over time, the ICTY discovered that after issuing its first several arrest warrants, securing arrests was the most critical and difficult issue of the system; local authorities experienced difficulties executing arrests.[45] Numerous state authorities did not cooperate with ICTY in executing arrest warrants because of the popularity or influence of the individual accused. Nationalism played a major role by inciting accusations that leaders unfairly distributed prosecutions against all parties to the conflict in the former Yugoslavia territories.[46]

Despite public involvement with several indictments, the ICTY efforts were successful relative to the other two case studies in this thesis. Although arrests were sometimes problematic, trials were swift and expeditious. The U.S. government's involvement peaked with the U.S. offering rewards of up to $5 million for information.[47] Although some of the accused fled the former Yugoslavia, it has generally only been a matter of time until capture because of the territories' successful diplomacy throughout the UN and neighboring affiliates.[48]

U.S. Military Sustainment in Yugoslavia

By 2001, over 16,000 U.S. Soldiers deployed to support the Bosnian conflict. The Army Service Component Command (ASCC) in Europe, U.S. Army Europe (USAREUR), executed Logistics Civilian Augmentation Program (LOGCAP) services to provide a wide spectrum of logistics including housing, food service, laundry operations, maintenance, shuttle bus services, and material handling equipment throughout the area of operation.[49] The mission in the Yugoslavia area rotated the 1st Armored Division and the 1st Infantry Division that required forward support battalions to support their logistics efforts. Division support commands and support brigades also provided sustainment support to divisions. Afterwards, the 2nd Armored Cavalry Regiment deployed to Bosnia with a Regimental Support Squadron to support Operation Joint Endeavor.

To streamline the sustainment effort in the Yugoslavia territories, support units conducted weekly materiel readiness reviews that facilitated the exchange of information on all classes of supply. This integration of numerous war fighting functions enabled the sustainment units to expeditiously fix any logistical problems. All leaders, especially the battalion executive officer and battalion motor officers, were held accountable. The U.S. military deployed into 24 base camps from where it could best observe the terms of the Dayton Accord. The sustainment of the U.S. military amassed to "a daily flow of three convoys and 12 air sorties carrying 75,000 meals, 192,000 gallons of water, 130,000 gallons of fuel, and 133 short tons of supplies."[50]

The entire deployment operation required 7,187 railcars, 1,408 cargo plane sorties, 373 trains, road transport assets (buses, trucks, and military vehicles), 441 buses, 42 military convoys, and 206 commercial truck convoys. The convoys transported over 9,000 passengers and 20,000 short tons of equipment.[51] In terms of fuel requirements throughout the duration of the operation, the Defense Energy Support Center, by January 1999, provided over 80 million gallons of fuel to Stabilization Force (SFOR) organizations in Bosnia, Croatia, and Hungary.[52]

Beyond the organic sustainment capabilities of the 1st Armored Division and 1st Infantry Division, Army operational contract support prescribed LOGCAP contracts with DynCorp and Brown and Root in the Bosnia Theater of operations. The U.S. military community once viewed the LOGCAP contractor as a money grubbing profiteer. Over time, the diligence of the LOGCAP community and action officers converted most U.S. military sustainment leadership to supporters that the LOGCAP program was an invaluable resource.[53]

U.S. military doctrine employs the Army's Title X responsibilities for support to other services as it inculcates the use of LOGCAP with the prospect to eliminate the normal big muscle movement required of military logisticians. The Yugoslavian case study proves the fidelity and utility of LOGCAP as professed by the USAREUR deputy commander and lead sustainment planners. LOGCAP became the logistics of choice because of the freedom and capabilities it provided the tactical commander.[54]

However, in Bosnia, planners oftentimes created duplication of effort with respects to transportation and maintenance. Because of the duplication, military personnel judged contractors as a waste of taxpayers' dollars. The Implementation Force's (IFOR) was the NATO-led multinational peacekeeping force in Bosnia and Herzegovina under a one-year mandate from December 1995 to December 1996 to support Operation Joint Endeavour. The IFOR's mission was "to successfully monitor the Former Warring Factions and enforce compliance with the Dayton Peace Accords."[55] The situation in Bosnia provided a special opportunity to collect sustainment experiences in and insights into the use of advanced information technology in a multifaceted, first-time-ever NATO-led coalition peace support operation.

Sustainment planners dealt with ripple effects of each of the technical sectors of the ETM that included security, governance, infrastructure, legal proceedings, and humanitarian aid. NATO, the United States, and its allies and the other coalition members of IFOR took on the challenge of transforming, in real time, a go-to-war designed military capability into one to support the needs of a complex peace operation."[56]"IFOR units worked with the OSCE on election preparations and human rights monitoring in OSCE field offices.

Military sustainment planners ensured logistics support to the ICTY in the investigation of war crimes. They also provided assistance to the UNHCR in the return of refugees and displaced persons."[57] To provide fidelity and mission command of sustainment efforts, "NATO and military leaders established an IFOR Commander for

Support (C-SPT) in Zagreb, Croatia."[58] The C-SPT's responsibilities included coordinating the sustainment, movements, medical, engineering, and contracting operations of the national logistic elements; and commanding selected IFOR units in support of the deployment, execution of peace implementation, and redeployment of IFOR. C-SPT was also the single point of contact for all IFOR matters pertaining to relations with the Croatian government.

Multinational and joint sustainment planners established the NATO Maintenance and Supply Agency (NAMSA) in a field office in Split, Croatia. They were responsible for all NATO common-funded contracting and contracting for all scarce resources in theater. They provided liaisons with C-SPT and the framework division. The command structure of sustainment to support policies offers a common thread for sustainment implications in North Korea. Although sustainment architecture exists in the KTO, NATO and other Asia-Pacific policy makers can drive the implementation of a force similar to the IFOR and C-SPT to augment the situation in the KTO that USFK and CFC will interface. The simplicity of a command structure can ease the burden of sustainment planners to inculcate concepts of sustainment nested with concepts of maneuver or stability operations. However, history shows that command structures in any theater of operations were complex, multi-dimensional, and not without regional challenges.

Case Study II Background: Ethiopia

Over the past fifty years, the Horn of Africa was the origin of several conflicts and negatively affected by numerous others.[59] While Ethiopia is the case study discussed, Eritrea is a particular episode in Ethiopian history with multi-dimensional implications that illustrate the operational environment. In 1991, Eritrea won independence after thirty

80

years of war. The global perception of Eritrea was one of idealistic opportunity. Eritrea, on the international stage, was a beacon of hope for a new Africa led by a man hailed as a revolutionary African statesman.[60] At the outset, Eritrea boasted low levels of corruption and crime, high levels of volunteerism, little tension among ethnic or confessional groups, relatively strong relations with neighbors, and no substantial debt.[61]

However, two decades later, Esayas Afeworki turned the world's hope into despair by misusing the trust of his people and betraying their confidence, executing dictatorial schemes.[62] The Eritrean People's Liberation Front (EPLF) followed a selective application of Marxist philosophy adapted to the context of the state's national liberation struggle.[63] By de facto independence in 1991 when the unpopular socialist regime in Addis Ababa fell, the EPLF built a national identity based on the identification of Eritrea as a central part of the African colonial experience.[64] During its first ten years as a sovereign state, Eritrea slid deeper into political repression and economic malaise.[65] Eritrean conflict led to tens of thousands dead, hundreds of thousands displaced, and economic instability.

This tension led to the Ethiopia-Eritrea war from 1998 to 2000 which led to no real border shifts and massive casualties. Ethiopia enjoyed friendly relations with Eritrea between 1991 and 1998; but a small border incident escalated into total war.[66] Fighting started in 1998 and ceased in 2000 when Ethiopian forces penetrated deep into Eritrea. Following binding arbitration that demarcated the border between the two territories, Eritrea accepted the outcome while Ethiopia aggressively objected.[67] Over time, these conflicts had U.S. sustainment planners speculating the direct use of terrorist tactics antagonistic to the government of Ethiopia, thereby creating an accessible environment that international terrorists can use for their own nefarious purposes.[68]

Security

Ethiopia hosts a number of states whose primary security concerns interlink in a regional security complex where national security is inherent.[69] Hence, interlinked conflicts induce security and sustainment planners to redefine sovereignty, the basis of citizenship, and the meaning of borders.[70]

Phase I: Initial Response

By 2005, the United Nations occupied a fifteen-mile-wide buffer zone along the Eritrean side of the border.[71] Ethiopia physically occupied the territory and had no incentive to resume fighting. Eritrea grew increasingly frustrated that Ethiopia did not accept the binding arbitration and internal challenges under the government of President Isaias Afwerki.[72] Concurrently, Ethiopia supported the Eritrean National Alliance (an Eritrean opposition group) while Eritrea supported anti-Ethiopian Somali and Oromo armed groups. Ethiopia's external threats included Islamic fundamentalism, particularly in Sudan. Ethiopia concluded that it required Sudanese support or neutrality as conflicts continued with Eritrea.[73] As alliances and regimes changed over time in the Horn of Africa, Ethiopia kept a watchful eye on the prospect of renewed efforts by the Sudan to export Islamic fundamentalism.[74]

Phase II: Transformation

From the perspective of the U.S. military, the outbreak of the Ethiopia-Eritrea war between its two major allies in an unstable environment was dreadful.[75] Then Assistant

Secretary of State for Africa, Susan Rice attempted to establish policies in an effort to control arms via agreement to settle diplomatically with Eritrean troops withdrawn and binding de-limitation of the border.[76] Demilitarization by both sides along the borders was also the key to U.S. policy. Ethiopia favored the plan, but Eritrea felt overrun by the US-Rwanda delegation. "The US-Rwanda proposal was formulated and presented in a manner that put the blame for the conflict on [Eritrea]."[77] Over time, the U.S. appreciated the significance of Djibouti as a logistical hub, sandwiched between Eritrea, Ethiopia and Somalia/Somaliland.[78]

The emergence of a Sudanese terrorist threat to Eritrea (Eritrean Islamic Jihad) generated urgency in providing aid. The commander of U.S. Central Command, General Tommy Franks visited Eritrea in the 1990s and Eritrea's chief of staff, General Sebhat Ephrem frequented visits to the United States to consult with Pentagon officials about regional security.[79] Each time Eritrea felt threatened, they employed their artillery against the Sudan (1994), then Yemen (1995), Djibouti (1996), and finally Ethiopia (1998). "Doing so helped to cement Eritrea's reputation as a volatile warrior-state and made the United States wary of getting too close, especially after Eritrea resumed the war with Ethiopia."[80]

Phase III: Fostering Sustainability

Between 1994 and 2001, Eritrea received $6 million in Foreign Military Financing and $2 million in International Military Education and Training assistance.[81] "There were three rounds of fighting before a cease-fire was reached: May–June 1998, February–March 1999, and May–June 2000."[82] Long-buried resentments and grievances erupted with an intensity never experienced in the area. This condition poisoned the

atmosphere for future reconciliation.

Figure 10. The Horn of Africa Map.

Source: U.S. Department of State, "Horn of Africa: Map," http://www.state.gov/p/af/rt/
hornofafrica/169532.htm (accessed February 15, 2014).

Governance and Participation

Early American efforts to mediate the conflict collapsed amid Eritrean charges

that the United States was tilting toward Ethiopia.[83] Relations worsened in 2002, as the

Asmara government blamed the U.S. for aiding Addis Ababa rather than pressuring it to follow through on its commitment to abide by the results of the arbitration.[84]

Phase I: Initial Response

Notwithstanding, the United States provided Eritrea with $71.6 million in humanitarian aid, including $65 million in food assistance and $3.36 million in refugee support, and $10.16 million in development assistance in 2003.[85] The prospect of more war coupled with the continuing suppression of democracy in Eritrea contributed to a chronically unstable environment in which terrorism will develop.[86] However, early-established policy and commitment from the United States induces the efforts for democracy and respect for basic civil and human rights in Eritrea. It is the key to moving dispute resolution forward and prevents the slide toward despotism.[87]

Phase II: Transformation

Ethiopia's 1994 constitution creates a federal multiparty system that accords unusual importance to the ethno-linguistic groupings in the country, stipulating that every nation has an unconditional right to self-determination, including the right to secession.[88] Since 1991, the Ethiopian People's Revolutionary Democratic Front (EPRDF) was the principal governing structure in Ethiopia. The EPRDF maintained close control over the military, the police, and the intelligence service. Although Ethiopia's system of government emphasized ethnic federalism and delegation of authority to the state governments, the EPRDF continues both subtly and sometimes not so subtly to retain complete control over the security forces.[89]

Throughout Ethiopia, U.S. leaders applied pressure. In October 1994, U.S. leaders created a task force by former Congressman Harry Johnson to try to mediate between the government and the opposition.[90] The US ambassador to Ethiopia, Irving Hicks unsuccessfully chaired diplomatic talks and the opposition boycotted the crucial 1995 elections.

U.S. officials concerned themselves over the human rights issues in Ethiopia. They also described Ethiopia as a 'Jekyll and Hyde' situation "because any US criticism of progress towards liberal democracy was more than offset by the view in Washington that Ethiopia was the key to America's regional policy, especially after the Somalia episode and with growing realization of Sudan's threat.[91] Meles Zenawi, Prime Minister of Ethiopia, visited Washington in 1994 where he met Clinton as the EPRDF and its allies easily won the 1995 elections.[92] In addition to the boycott of the opposition parties, there was a growth of Islamist activity. Constituents outraged over the attack on President Mubarak in Addis Ababa in June 1995. The U.S. had to balance the threat to its ally from the possible growth of Islamist violence."[93]

Phase III: Fostering Sustainability

During the Global War on Terror, President Bush praised Ethiopia's assistance and assured Meles that the United States would work closely with him to deter any terrorist plots against Ethiopia.[94] Speaking in Addis Ababa, Secretary of Defense Donald Rumsfeld warned that the Horn of Africa had provided a home for Al Qaeda. During a visit to Ethiopia in early 2003, Major General John F. Sattler, commander of the Combined Joint Task Force-Horn of Africa (CJTF-HOA), commented that Ethiopia was a valuable partner to disrupt terrorism against coalition partners.[95] General John Abizaid,

United States Central Command (USCENTCOM) commander, visited Addis Ababa in July 2003 and February 2004.

In Ethiopia, CJTF-HOA trained the Ethiopian National Defense Forces at the Hurso training camp, northwest of Dire Dawa infantry tactics against terrorism.[96] CJTF-HOA wanted to establish three new Ethiopian antiterrorism companies with a temporary training facility called Camp Unity at Hurso to carry out the program. Other training included medical and veterinary civic action programs and school refurbishment in the area.[97]

Humanitarian Assistance and Social Well-Being

Since the early 1990s, the U.S. military has become much more sophisticated in its approach to cooperation with humanitarian organizations. One vignette was the areas surrounding Ethiopia, Eritrea, and the Horn of Africa.

Phase I: Initial Response

Military and government agencies have sponsored (or participated in) a variety of conferences, colloquia and exercises designed to effect better cooperation. Throughout the U.S. military, the United States European Command (USEUCOM) designed semi-permanent planning teams containing representatives from such organizations. USCENTCOM conducts an annual symposium to assess mechanisms to facilitate cooperation. That said, the Horn of Africa was one area where much more could be done to facilitate effective humanitarian and peace interventions.[98]

Phase II: Transformation

As a poor and populous country, contemporary Ethiopia receives roughly $900 million in aid per year, according to a UN advisor to Secretary General Kofi Annan. The UN Development Program concluded that aid to Ethiopia increased from $605 million in 1997 to $1.937 billion in 2003.[99] Ethiopia benefits from the $100 million U.S.-financed East Africa Counterterrorism Initiative (EACTI).

Phase III: Fostering Sustainability

Starting in 2003, the EACTI "provides military training for border and coastal security, programs to strengthen capacity-building, and assistance for regional efforts to combat terrorist financing and train police."[100] Coupled with the EACTI, the global humanitarian effort ensures that Ethiopia continues to receive substantial aid to promote stability in the region. Ethiopia received the equivalent of nearly 12 percent of its gross national income in humanitarian aid.[101]

Economic Stabilization and Infrastructure

In Ethiopia, problems pertaining to the logistical support of industrial enterprises lack standards. The Ethiopian industry lacks mature supplies with many kinds of raw materials, especially with agricultural produce.[102]

Phase I: Initial Response

Ethiopia is one of the poorest countries in the world as only half of the population has access to minimal levels of health care and only a quarter has access to safe drinking water.[103] Ethiopia has not produced enough food to feed its population since the late 1960s. To exacerbate conditions, "Ethiopia's population of 72 million will double every twenty-three years."[104] The trifecta of poverty, structural food deficits, and a high population growth rate place increasing pressure on Ethiopia's ability to remain politically stable.[105]

Phase II: Transformation

The World Bank cancelled most of Ethiopia's debt. Although Ethiopia spent a great deal during the 1998–2000 war, it purchased many of its needs with cash and quickly cut back military expenditures at the end of the war.[106] This implies a lack of industrialization or a developed infrastructure, as other forms of trade unionism were generally weak in Ethiopia.[107] War inhibited any positive developments in Ethiopia, setting the developmental process many years back, as the economic and human loss of the war was extremely high.[108]

Phase III: Fostering Sustainability

The war between Eritrea and Ethiopia devastated all aspects of social and economic life, reversing the positive gains Eritrea made during the post-independence period. The war affected 2.2 million people of whom, "1.1 million (one-third) of the population) were displaced, many lives were lost, and led to a massive destruction of public and private assets, a collapse in agricultural production, and severe economic stress."[109] The structural damage of the war affected the economic infrastructure of the state building process.[110] The 1998-2000 war diverted hard-earned income and revenue to the war effort and the maintenance of a huge army able to withstand the external threat during the two years.[111]

Numerous actors, during the transitional period, accused the EPRDF of manipulation of the rule of law and free elections. During election periods, opposition parties made unexpected and spectacular gains in elections to sweep with a substantial majority. During re-tabulation efforts, a suspected EPRDF break in the chain of control of ballot boxes enraged the opposition who contested the results.

Phase I: Initial Response

Leaders initiated a Special Prosecutor's Office in 1992 to try members of the old regime. Several years later, hundreds of people were still languishing in detention awaiting trial. Public confidence derailed and for ordinary civilians there were questions about justice. International monitors such as Amnesty International and Human Rights Watch/Africa compiled reports of apparent injustices, as did the newly formed Ethiopian Human Rights Council."[112]

Phase II: Transformation

Coupled with the delays in trial proceedings and mismanagement of indictments, the EPRDF interjected in suspected ballot manipulation in 1994 when "fresh elections at federal and regional levels marked the final chapter in the transitional period."[113] In the early 1990s, the U.S. supported the EPRDF. The public questioned the outcome of the 2005 and 2010 elections largely because of the EPRDF's manipulation of ballots.

Phase III: Fostering Sustainability

The EPRDF appeared in charge, but the holistic approach to the democratic process was questionable.[114] The situation regarding human rights was central and there were some disturbing developments from the outset. Long delays undermined public confidence in the rule of law. Regardless, the EPRDF was a step ahead in the direction away from Mengistu Haile Mariam's autocratic rule of the communist military junta in the 1980s and episodes in genocide.

U.S. Military Sustainment in Ethiopia

Because of the emerging situation in the Horn of Africa, on 6 February 2007, President George W. Bush announced that the United States will create a new military command for Africa, to be known as United States Africa Command (USAFRICOM).[115] During the 1998-2000 Ethiopia-Eritrea conflict, USEUCOM and USCENTCOM split responsibilities to sustain any use of the U.S. military. Intermittently post-war, CJTF-HOA played a direct role in planning stability operations in the region.

The demand signal was there to create and established a permanent presence known as USAFRICOM. Instantly, the U.S. took initiative with numerous refugee and humanitarian relief efforts in Ethiopia. Through the coordination of the Joint Interagency Coordination Group (JIACG), USAFRICOM leaders successfully synchronized humanitarian relief and peace operations with coalition partners, non-governmental organizations (NGOs) and Private Voluntary Organizations (PVOs). These humanitarian organizations played substantial and indispensable roles in addressing some of the root causes of instability.[116]

Inherent in the formulation of a newly established geographic combatant command is its sustainment challenges. Regional solutions in the Horn of Africa to approaching conflicts links with the U.S. willingness to set conditions through early guarantees of funding and logistic support to organizations prepared to head off crises in

91

early stages. In peace operations in Africa, the United States should be willing on short notice to deploy forces as first responders for temporary peace enforcement operations.[117] With the new regionally aligned forces concept under the auspices of the U.S. Army, USAFRICOM can enable its joint and multinational sustainment planner's prescriptive plans and enhanced fidelity to respond to forecasted consumption ratios and commodity management.

In 2007, AFRICOM joined CJTF-HOA as plans proceeded until AFRICOM became operational by the end of 2008.[118] By the end of 2012, 3,500 troops and representatives from 14 countries served at the CJTF-HOA Headquarters at Camp Lemonnier, Djibouti."[119] According to Obama's Strategy toward Sub-Saharan Africa, while continuing to lead the world in response to humanitarian crises in Africa, the U.S. will promote and bring to scale resilience policies and programs. The U.S., through all the instruments of national power, prevents the weakening or collapse of local economies, protect livestock, promote access to clean water, and invest in programs that reduce community-level vulnerability to enhance regional stability.[120]

The aftermath of the Ethiopia-Eritrea conflict and throughout the Horn of Africa ingrained the U.S. commitment to the region in light of the terrorist attacks on the World Trade Center. CJTF-HOA spearheaded the effort as the U.S. hunted terrorists not only in the USCENTCOM area of responsibility, but also in the Horn of Africa. To sustain the President's declaration of the Global War on Terror, the United States' facilities at Djibouti's Camp Lemonnier became its sole permanent base on the African continent.[121]

Djibouti, over time, became a sustainment hub for US and allied operations in East Africa and the Arabian Peninsula. Kuwait and Qatar were the principal sustainment hubs for the Arabian Peninsula as the sustainment planning effort also incorporated Djibouti as the launching pad for drone surveillance and attacks. NATO inculcated Djibouti as the logistics hub for anti-piracy and other multilateral missions in the region. The AFRICOM and CJTF-HOA sustainment lead officer involves other countries, such as France, that retain almost 2,000 troops in Djibouti.

Case Study III Background: Haiti

For 35 seconds the earthquake in Haiti reduced a nation—already struggling with the historical weight of slavery, underdevelopment, imperialism, and intense internal divisions—to rubble.[122] One in seven Haitians were homeless while roughly 316,000 people lost their lives.[123] Leaders such as former president Bill Clinton saw an opportunity to undo the damage wrought by policies he championed as president. In the first week, private US citizens contributed $275 million, mostly to large NGOs like the Red Cross, reaching $1 billion by 1 March.[124] Sixty percent of US households and more than 80 percent of African American families contributed to the Haiti earthquake response, despite feeling the pinch from the recession.[125]

Security

In 2004, a revolt began in northern Haiti where Jean-Bertrand Aristide was the leader of the country. The rebellion eventually reached Port-au-Prince, the Haitian capital. Aristide went into exile, whereupon the United Nations became involved and stationed peacekeepers in Haiti. Security became an issue over time because of regional instability. The 2010 earthquake exacerbated the situation as it created an extraordinary influx of people, estimated at 690,000, "by providing them shelter, a plate of food, and effective support."[126]

Phase I: Initial Response

After 15 years of UN missions from 1995 to 2010, the international community showed no sign of changing course in Haiti. Despite the presence of United Nations Stabilization Mission in Haiti (MINUSTAH), the country has not really restored a climate of stability and security. A history of conflict and strife plagued Haiti's security and the earthquake of 2010 complicated Haiti's development.

Phase II: Transformation

Haiti kept the attention of the US foreign policy community because of constant concern over illegal migration. Numerous illegal immigration attempts highlighted the periodic outflow towards south Florida of large numbers of desperate boatpeople. Every American president from Jimmy Carter to George W. Bush has had to confront the immigration hot rail of US policy towards Haiti and toward Haitians.[127] United States Southern Command (USSOUTHCOM) has the responsibility to oversee Haiti's regional stability and security in the interests of the U.S.

Phase III: Fostering Sustainability

USSOUTHCOM is the organization charged with the American response to Haitian refugees seeking entry to the United States, specifically with Coast Guard interdiction on the high seas that results in deportation to Haiti. There is also ongoing interest in Haiti's role in narco-trafficking. "The weak state is located in the crosshairs of a drug-trafficking network that originates in Colombia, ends in North America, fuels corruption and violence in Haiti and funnels approximately 8 percent of the cocaine consumed annually in the United States."[128]

On 13 January 2010, under the direction of USSOUTHCOM, elements of the Department of Defense arrived to assist the Government of Haiti and the United States Embassy. That day, the 1st Special Operations Wing arrived and reopened Toussaint Louverture International Airport, while the United States Coast Guard Higgins and United States military aircraft began delivering relief supplies and conducted non-combatant evacuation operations of American citizens.[129] Recognizing the need to establish a command and control element for the rapidly growing force, USSOUTHCOM established Headquarters, Joint Task Force - Haiti to conduct Humanitarian Assistance and Disaster Relief operations in support of the United States Agency for International Development (USAID) and Non-Governmental Organizations (NGOs), in order to mitigate suffering and save lives.[130]

Governance and Participation

Haitians sought a participatory democracy from the brutal thirty-year Duvalier dictatorship in 1986. Even through 2010, "through many public declarations, press conferences . . . daily demonstrations, citizens are asserting that it is their right to be formally brought into decision making."[131] The Haitian constituents felt absent from the political process as Haitian leaders made decisions without any votes from the people.

Phase I: Initial Response

"Despite their advocacy, the Haitian people, together with their government, have been bypassed in the planning and oversight of how aid money is spent and in reconstruction policies."[132] Coupled with the 2010 earthquake, UN Secretary-General Ban Ki-moon described the process as an exercise in nation building on an unprecedented scale and scope not seen in generations. However, the Haitian voice was lost amid the political and opportunistic transnational actors.

Phase II: Transformation

On 15 April the Haitian Parliament formally gave up its powers over finances and reconstruction to a foreign-led *Commission Interimaire pour la Reconstruction d'Haiti* (CIRH) for "the next 18 months with mandates to direct the post-earthquake reconstruction of Haiti through the $9.9 billion in pledges of international aid, including approving policies, projects, and budgeting."[133] UN Special Envoy and former U.S. President Bill Clinton led the CIRH. "The only accountability or oversight measure is Haitian President René Préval's veto power."[134] Few expected Preval to use the veto power and many accused Preval for his weak disaster response.

Phase III: Fostering Sustainability

Haiti's prolonged history of unstable governance and weak institutions have made the country seem like it is perpetually dependent upon foreign assistance. The nature and character of this assistance changed since MINUSTAH launched in 2004, when for the first time Latin American countries have been leaders of the effort to help Haiti become a stable country. The Haiti earthquake opened a new chapter for understanding "the complex interplay between international cooperation and state building, especially the new ways of crafting such cooperation and how different kinds of actors (international institutions, states and non-governmental organizations) can act cohesively and constructively.[135]

Under the Bush administration, the policy towards Haiti was largely one of estrangement, "with most bilateral assistance suspended, humanitarian aid redirected through non-governmental organizations and pressure exerted on multilateral donors to replicate this approach."[136] A new US approach towards Haiti under the Obama administration includes opportunities for strengthening prospects and improving relations for stability, democratization and more effective support.[137]

Humanitarian Assistance and Social Well-Being

Without doubt, humanitarian relief programs that provide food to displaced and impoverished people was a top priority.[138]

Phase I: Initial Response

After the 2010 earthquake, 1.5 million of its 9.7 million people had to find refuge after displacement in the aftermath of January's earthquake. Furthermore, a much higher number of the 78 percent of Haiti's entire population received earnings of less than two dollars a day. Without homes, the U.S. government responded with the prospect of unceasing poverty accompanied by hunger, disease and malnutrition. USSOUTHCOM responded with the formulation of JTF-H and JTF-Logistics Haiti.

Phase II: Transformation

By 2012, a competing priority, was to focus on medium- and long-term development needs that included support of efforts for Haitians to grow their own food. The aforementioned government development strategies dwelled on the dilemma of

Haiti's extreme vulnerability to global increases in the cost of imported food and fuel that exacerbate widespread citizen suffering."[139] During this period, the NGOs and USAID saved tens of thousands of lives and humanized conditions in some of the makeshift camps in the metropolitan area, Léogâne, and Petit-Goâve.

Phase III: Fostering Sustainability

Many observers reported serious imbalances and uneven distribution of aid, which focused primarily on the central regions that enjoyed a higher visibility with the media and international coverage.[140] "The injection of funds through Cash for Work programs failed to support activities and did not bring about new leadership or new social commitment."[141]

Economic Stabilization and Infrastructure

Haiti should operate under a new economic paradigm in the aftermath of the earthquake, one "that breaks free of unfair trade rules under which food and many other basics are imported, and a coveted job is in a sweatshop."[142]

Phase I: Initial Response

Disaster capitalists flocked to Haiti with the aim to build contracts early for maximum exposure and profitability.[143] As an example of disaster capitalism, "former US presidential candidate and retired General Wesley Clark [promoted] . . . InnoVida Holdings, a Miami-based company that had pledged to donate 1,000 foam-core panel-built houses for Haiti's homeless."[144] Disaster capitalists focused on profiting in the new market for Haiti's reconstruction effort, inhibiting some of the goodwill by USAID and the U.S. government.

Phase II: Transformation

NGOs played a central role in the aftermath of the 2010 earthquake. The reconstruction project reflected a growing problem of contracting non-Haitian firms, as well as an increasing trend in no-bid contracts given to US companies. The role of the NGO pronounced an increased role in shaping humanitarian coverage, with some organizations having closer ties to media outlets than others.

Phase III: Fostering Sustainability

Media scholar Natalie Fenton has faulted this phenomenon for increasingly shallow coverage of serious issues, and the dominance of more powerful NGOs in mediating the narrative that gets disseminated.[145] Despite the plethora of large multi-contingency contribution by national governments, NGOs contributed more significantly to both solicitation of aid for the rescue efforts and on-the-ground rescue efforts. The role of the NGO in dealing with internally displaced persons and refugees is indispensable.

Justice and Reconciliation

Phase I: Initial Response

The country does not control its borders with the Dominican Republic and has not drastically reduced the transit of drugs. MINUSTAH has already cost nearly $3.7 billion between June 2004 and October 2010."[146] "MINUSTAH remains a powerful force in imposing decisions in one sense or another that are not in the interests of the majority of the population."[147]

Phase II: Transformation

"On November 28, 2010, Haitians went to the polls to elect a new president . . . most important, the very legitimacy of the election was called into question after more than a dozen political parties were excluded from the election—including Haiti's most popular political party"[148] The ban on Fanmi Lavalas was analogous to excluding the two major political parties in the United States. Furthermore, there existed no effective measures to ensure that thousands of voters without identification cards or their homes destroyed following the January 12 earthquake would have the means to vote.[149]

Phase III: Fostering Sustainability

Over the long run, there were major problems in the conduct of the elections and the tallying of votes. "With so many millions of residents displaced by the earthquake, and many missing most of their possessions, including voting cards, ensuring that all of Haiti's eligible voters could participate in the elections was a gargantuan task."[150] Affected Haitians who wanted to vote did not have the means without identification cards.

U.S. Military Sustainment in Haiti

At the peak of Operation Unified Response (OUR) in Haiti, JTF-H comprised of over 22,000 service members, 58 aircraft, and 23 ships. JTF-H and Operation Unified Response lasted nearly five months.[151] Joint Task Force-Haiti assumed responsibility for all U.S. forces and directed operations in USSOUTCHOM's directives. Instantly, the XVIII Airborne Corps assault command post, 2nd Brigade Combat Team (2/82 Infantry Brigade Combat Team), 82nd Airborne Division, deployed with 58 fixed-wing and rotary-wing aircraft with elements of the amphibious ready groups. The key sustainment

assets included the 2/82 IBCT's organic sustainment assets of a brigade support battalion.

In the first 100 days of Operation Unified Response, the U.S. Agency for International

Development (USAID) was the lead Federal agency for disaster response to the Haitian

earthquake. In total, U.S. Southern Command and JTF-H supplied 680,000 gallons of

water, 2,900,000 humanitarian rations packages, 17,000,000 pounds of bulk food,

2,700,000 meals-ready to eat, and 73,300 emergency radios.[152]

U.S. Southern Command supplied 149,000 pounds of medical supplies, cleared

12,724 cubic yards of rubble in city streets, and treated 9,758 personnel.[153] JTF-H also

consisted of elements of the 3rd Expeditionary Sustainment Command, which

collectively led efforts through the emergency phase and into the sustained relief phase of

OUR. Additionally, the whole-of-government approach to respond to Haiti's aid include

the Joint Forces Command, Northern Command, European Command, and to mobilize

personnel to augment JTF-H with required specialties.

The U.S. Navy's hospital ship U.S. Naval Ship *Comfort*, equipped with surgical

operating teams and orthopedic surgeons, arrived to support OUR. 2/82 IBCT supported

multiple interagency humanitarian aid distribution efforts in the most severely influenced

areas of the Haitian capital, Port-au-Prince. JTF-H and JTF-Logistics Haiti established

sixteen distribution sites to provide food, water, and medical care."[154]

Photo Removed Due to Copyright Restrictions

Figure 11. U.S. Ship *Fort McHenry* and U.S. Ship *Carter Hall* arrive at the New Hope
Mission in Bonel, Haiti, 19 January 2010.

Source: Ken Keen et al., "Foreign Disaster Response: Joint Task Force-Haiti
Observations," *Military Review* (November-December 2010): 88.

Although more than 230,000 people died from the 2010 earthquake, the abundant
and timely medical assistance provided by the multinational effort saved thousands of
lives. Sustainment was the most significant challenge facing the U.S. military and the
international community in the initial emergency phase. Overall, the U.S. military's
logistics response was robust and proactive.

Sustainment planners have difficulties to quantify gallons of fuel and short tons of
material when given an incomplete situational awareness in the emergency phase, as was
the case in the initial phase of OUR. An absence in the early phase of OUR of unified and
integrated logistics mission command to synchronize, anticipate, and integrate the overall
logistics effort led to sustainment gaps in force flow of personnel, equipment, and
supplies into Haiti.[155]

Case Study I: Yugoslavia—Applications to North Korea

During North Korean regime collapse, like Yugoslavia, a UN protection force can supplement CFC and USFK with UNPAs established. CFC will enforce exclusion zones and military personnel will mobilize to react to the North Korean threat and millions of IDPs. Over time, peace agreements will be established such as the Dayton Peace Agreements, but in full effort to unify Korea United Nations Security Resolutions will pass to facilitiate peace agreements and regional stability. CFC and USFK employs early protection policies for three million refugees and provide first responder support for humanitarian aid packages. UNHCR will become involved in the NATO mission to honor the ROK and NATO cooperation partnership. The North Korean military damages infrastructure as new economic sanctions develop for economic recovery plans. Any war crimes by North Korean leadership will try in court with emerging international tribunals.

Table 5.   ETM Goals Matrix: Yugoslavia

Technical Sector	Initial Response	Transformation	Fostering Sustainability
Security	UNPROFOR & UNPAs established	Delivered relief supplies Established exclusion zones	20,000 troops mobilized: commitment
Governance & Participation	Dayton Peace Agreements established	Ethnic cleansing activities	Established governance with UNSCR 836
Humanitarian Assistance & Social Well-Being	Early defined protection policy for refugees	Humanitarian aid for refugees employed as part of information operations	UNHCR heavily involved in the NATO mission
Economic Stabilization & Infrastructure	1999 Air War with Serbia damaged economy	Economic embargoes and sanctions led to increased violence	After violence, U.S. got involved in economic recovery plans
Justice & Reconciliation	International Criminal Tribunal started actions against war crimes	Crimes between 1991-2001 were addressed in court	Public became involved to seize criminals after witnessing functional due process

Source: Created by Author.

103

Case Study II: Ethiopia—Applications to North Korea

During North Korean regime collapse, the United Nations can establish a buffer zone enforced by CFC and USFK. A ceasefire agreement will insure stability in the region. Political parties in North Korea will dissolve and diplomatic authorities will negotiate the means to unify Korea. The poor economic conditions in North Korea, like Ethiopia, can have a negative impact on unification efforts. Swift legal proceedings will lead to increased public confidence. PACOM, CFC, and USFK will absorb humanitarian ration and shelter plans for three million IDPs. The World Bank will assess North Korea's economic posture and debt. Post-conflict reconstruction can be cumbersome depending on the catastrophic effects and losses of combat and armed conflict. Citizenship transition services will be incorporated to ensure long-term integration of North Koreans to establish new sovereignty under the ROK constitution.

Table 6.   ETM Goals Matrix: Ethiopia

Technical Sector	Initial Response	Transformation	Fostering Sustainability
Security	UN established buffer zone	Eritrea continued to attack Ethiopia	Ceasefire agreement reached
Governance & Participation	US committed to democracy in Ethiopia; established policy early	EPRDF stranglehold over Ethiopia	CJTF-HOA leadership inculcated Ethiopia armed forces on GWOT
Humanitarian Assistance & Social Well-Being	EUCOM/CENTCOM established plans for HA; Ethiopia receives $900 mil / year	Aid rose to over $1 bil by 2003; receives $100 mil in EACTI	EACTI conducts military training to strengthen regional efforts; 1.1 million IDPs
Economic Stabilization & Infrastructure	Poor country leads to political instability	World bank cancelled Ethiopia's debt, infrastructure still dilapidated	State-building process hindered because of devastating losses during war
Justice & Reconciliation	Special Prosecutor's Office established: results of trial lagged with many in detention for long periods	1994 elections started but EPRDF held stranglehold	Long delays undermined public confidence in the rule of law

Source: Created by Author.

Case Study III: Haiti—Applications to North Korea

North Korean regime collapse will induce three million IDPs and refugees with several other factions departing in various different directions. The prospect of a unifed Korea can take decades or generations to erase the Juche ideology. Information operations is the key to winning the indigenous population's confidence through humanitarian aid and packages. Inequality and imbalances in the distribution of aid will lead to restlessness and potential violence. Relationships with UNHCR, intergovernmental organizations (IGOs), PVOs, and NGOs are key components for successful CFC, USFK, and PACOM planning.

Table 7.   ETM Goals Matrix: Haiti

Technical Sector	Initial Response	Transformation	Fostering Sustainability
Security	Haiti's security and the earthquake of 2010 complicated Haiti's development	USSOUTHCOM involved with illegal immigration	Crosshairs of a drug-trafficking network undermines fidelity in security
Governance & Participation	Haitan people bypassed in oversight in policies; fresh memories of dictatorship	Foreign-led Commission Interimaire pour la Reconstruction d'Haiti (CIRH)	White House Policy: improving relations and strengthening prospects for stability for Haiti
Humanitarian Assistance & Social Well-Being	1.5 million IDPs; activated humanitarian aid	Humanitarian aid saved tens of thousands of lives and humanized conditions	Serious imbalances and inequality in the distribution of aid; CFW program corruption led to lower confidence
Economic Stabilization & Infrastructure	Disaster capitalists were flocking to Haiti in a 'gold rush' for contracts	Growing problem of contracting non-Haitian firms	Dominance of more powerful NGOs creates a freeze on economic development
Justice & Reconciliation	MINUSTAH remains a powerful force in imposing decisions	Very legitimacy of elections was called into question	major problems in the conduct of the elections and the tallying of votes.

Source: Created by Author.

Summary of ETM Analysis

The following table reflects the trends across the three case studies to use as a reference when applying sustainment considerations in the KTO. Sustainment planners can use this ETM analysis and lessons learned from Yugoslavia (USEUCOM area of responsibility), Ethiopia (USAFRICOM area of responsibility), and Haiti (USSOUTHCOM) area of responsibility to apply to the KTO (USPACOM area of responsibility). Despite the geographic and cultural differences, many of the doctrinal placements remain stable and flexible enough to warrant consideration.

Table 8.   Summary of Case Studies/Trends

Technical Sector	Initial Response	Transformation	Fostering Sustainability
Security	IDPs complicate development of countries; UN established buffer zone; UNPROFOR & UNPAs established	Involvement with illegal immigration; Continued attacks between territories; Delivered relief supplies Established exclusion zones	Crosshairs of a drug-trafficking network undermines fidelity in security; Ceasefire agreement reached; troops mobilized and stabilized to honor commitments
Governance & Participation	People bypassed in oversight in policies; fresh memories of dictatorship; US committed to democracy; established policy early; Peace Agreements established	Foreign-led Commissions to provide oversight; political parties stranglehold over the nation; families reconciling after decades of displacement	White House Policy: improving relations and strengthening prospects for stability; GCC leadership inculcates new allies to U.S. foreign policy; new UNSCR to establish governance
Humanitarian Assistance & Social Well-Being	~3 million IDPs; activated humanitarian aid; establish yearly aid in hundreds of millions of dollars per year; Early defined protection policy for refugees	Humanitarian aid saved tens of thousands of lives and humanized conditions; aid rise to over $1 billion; Humanitarian aid for refugees employed as part of information operations	Serious imbalances and inequality in the distribution of aid; CFW program corruption led to lower confidence; conduct military training to stabilize region; UNHCR heavily involved in the mission
Economic Stabilization & Infrastructure	Disaster capitalists flock to scene in a 'gold rush' for contracts; country remains poor and in shock; Destruction of war damaged economy	Growing problem of foreign firms looking to profit; World Bank becomes involved; Economic embargoes and sanctions led to increased violence	Dominance of more powerful NGOs creates a freeze on economic development; State-building process hindered because of devastating losses during war; U.S. got involved in economic recovery plans
Justice & Reconciliation	Political parties remain a powerful force in imposing decisions; Special Prosecutor's Office established: results of trial lagged with many in detention for long periods; International Criminal Tribunal started actions against war crimes	Very legitimacy of elections was called into question; elections begin but political parties seek dominance; war crimes to be addressed in court	Major problems in the conduct of the elections and the tallying of votes; Long delays undermined public confidence in the rule of law; Public became involved to seize criminals after witnessing functional due process

Source: Created by Author.

Applying the ETM Analysis to Sustainment in North Korea

The ETM matrix is not a sustainment requirements generating model. However, the analysis sheds light to military sustainment planners the potential of new requirements. Its thoroughness forces the military sustainment planner to plan for other variables that U.S. military sustainment forecasting tools (Operations Logistics Planner Version 8.0 and Logistics Estimate Worksheet) do not directly calculate.

The KTO hosts an expeditionary sustainment command (ESC) or the 19th ESC. As prescribed in the case study of Yugoslavia, the C-SPT was the sustainment mission command headquarters to streamline sustainment operation and coordinate with other nations and services. As the KTO develops to one of offensive operations and refugee assistance, the prospect of split-based sustainment operations is essential as in the case of Yugoslavia, where numerous other nations participated in regional stability. The Allied Command Europe Rapid Reaction Corps was the land component command from the British forces. The Allied Command Europe Rapid Reaction Corps Support Command was the Forward Commander and positioned in Split, Croatia. He was responsible for reporting movement into theater to C-SPT. The sustainment planners in USFK and CFC must be cognizant of the other nations' support structures that may deploy to the KTO under USPACOM directives.

In Bosnia, three National Support Elements (NSE) supported stability operations: the French in Ploce, Croatia, the United States in Kaposvar, Hungary, and the British in Split, Croatia. Under the IFOR staff structure, all troop-contributing nations used the national logistics stovepipes to support their forces in Bosnia with the chief of sustainment synchronizing efforts across the command to achieve strategic objectives.

The ROK and US may be the only NSEs in the KTO as other nations deploy an NSE in combination with other nations. In Yugoslavia, C-SPT was the responsible agent to serve as the Commander in Chief of IFOR's logistics commander. The C-SPT equivalent in the KTO is essentially the 19th ESC.

To complement other nations and services, a Joint Task Force-Logistics Korea as the one employed in JTF-Logistics Haiti will have to execute mission command of streamlined sustainment objectives to ensure the continuous sustainment of millions of gallons of fuel and short tons of ammunition. As in the case of a prospective JTF-Logistics Korea, C-SPT set up the roles of the Engineer Coordination Center, the Joint Logistics Operations Center, the Joint Movement Control Center, the Medical Coordination Center, and the Theater Contracting Coordination Center. C-SPT's efforts to sustain each of the five technical sectors in the post-Tito Yugoslavian conflicts were a positive way in which to address multinational logistics.[156]

The friction experienced by sustainment initiatives in the Yugoslavia area developed because of reception, staging, and onward movement of forces into the theater of operations. The forward presence of forces in the KTO mitigates such friction. In Yugoslavia, USAREUR provided the administrative and logistical support at the intermediate staging base (ISB).[157] The equivalent to USAREUR in the KTO is Eighth U.S. Army (EUSA), as an established field army to conduct similar procedures such as facilitation of an ISB in the KTO. The resident Army Service Component Command (ASCC) involved in the KTO is U.S. Army Pacific that delegates many of those responsibilities to EUSA. For all of PACOM, U.S. Army Pacific is the ASCC, but within the KTO, the ASCC is EUSA.

In Bosnia, the UN inculcated an International Police Task Force that relied on the U.S. military for many forms of support ranging from radio maintenance, diesel fuel, medical care, water, rations, showers, and maps.[158] The prospect of a similar IPTF in the KTO is not unlikely as sustainment planners can anticipate the logistics required to support internment and resettlement activities. The ROK can also procure many of these capabilities in conjunction with USFK and EUSA. Over time, IFOR's mission concluded and NATO created SFOR to conduct stability operations during IFOR's transition.

In the Yugoslavia case study, the U.S. military combat service support elements arrival at the Bosnia Theater of operations was late and often fragmented which put IFOR at a disadvantage from the outset.[159] After several months, IFOR established a stable logistics communication structure, operational supply support areas, and diminished supply backlogs. The forward U.S. military presence in the KTO eliminates most of the friction inherent in reception, staging, and onward movement.

Reducing the U.S. military presence in the KTO in the event of North Korean regime collapse will induce difficulties in establishing a strong sustainment structure capable of providing support to the KTO. Another example of strong sustainment architecture in the KTO is the established framework of the Standard Army Management Information Systems, such as the Standard Army Maintenance System, Standard Army Retail Supply System, and the Integrated Logistics Analysis Program. In the Bosnia area of operations, IFOR suffered a backlog as the C-SPT spent several weeks to gain stable functionality for all the STAMIS systems.

The U.S. government's reliance on contractors, especially during conflicts and stability operations is concrete and historically strong. In Bosnia, sustainment planners instilled contractor support and related logistic support arrangements for military use to ensure continuity of service in a hostile environment.[160] The use of contractors during North Korean regime collapse is inevitable and welcome to insure fidelity of resources and filling any sustainment gaps in a complex operational environment with offensive operations and three million IDPs.

In the former Yugoslavia, by 2003, SFOR increased efforts to detain war crimes suspects and provided logistical support for internationally monitored elections, and provided limited assistance for refugee resettlement.[161] The ETM technical sectors displayed here proves that a sustainment planner must consider all facets of the instruments of national power to achieve strategic objectives. A sustainment planner can no longer just concern him or herself with the tactical mission as the aperture widens to support other U.S. governmental objectives resides on sustainment functions such as resourcing and providing life support.

In response to the Dayton Proximity Talks on 16 November 1995, the Commanding General of USAREUR directed logistics planners to order the railhead trains to distribute and transport materiel. At the same time, USAREUR started coordination with LOGCAP and drafted statements of work for operational contractor support.[162] As in the case of the KTO, LOGCAP will play a fundamental role in the establishment of distribution and transportation and many other logistics functions. The sustainment planner can achieve gaps in support with constraints, restraints, or shortfalls.

To gain an appreciation of the task to sustain the National Support Element at Taszar, Hungary in December 1995, the sustainment planner had to figure out how to support USAREUR (Forward), 21st Theater Army Area Command (Forward), Logistics support element, 19th Transportation Company, 27th Transportation Battalion (Movement Control), 266th Finance Command, 29th Area Support Group, 51st Ordnance Battalion, 95th Military Police Battalion (-), 28th Transportation Battalion, 191st Ordnance Battalion (-), 330th Rear Tactical Operations Center (Presidential Selective Reserve Call-Up), 16th Corps Support Group (Forward), 1st Personnel Command (Forward), 30th Medical Brigade (Rear)(-), 7th Signal Brigade (-), and Task Force Eagle quartering parties.[163]

The number of organizations and organic support to one NSE, combined with two others can become complicated. The solution to absorb the shortfalls is for the sustainment planner to analyze LOGCAP to turn things over when military forces culminate. The U.S. military turns to the U.S. Army for Title X responsibilities to provide logistics support. In the Bosnia Theater, "USAREUR Headquarters (Forward) commanded the NSE and ISB, under which fell the 21st Theater Sustainment Command (Forward) and the area support group responsible for commanding and maintaining the installations."[164]

In the same light as USAREUR, EUSA or USARPAC may provide all logistical support to conduct Title 10 responsibilities for all American forces in the KTO. To mitigate unanticipated requirements, setting up an ISB lessens the logistical load on sustainment planners, as the ISB in Hungary lessened the logistical load on the USAREUR planners. Over time, USAREUR sustainment planners admitted that "turning things over to LOGCAP [was] a smart thing to do. It saved force structure and . . . money in the long run."[165] LOGCAP can fill the gaps to reduce the dependence of uniformed

111

services. An Army Field Support Brigade headquarters manages LOGCAP operations in Daegu, ROK.

In the Ethiopia Theater of operations, Djibouti became a logistical hub catered to military and naval cooperation among and beyond NATO and EU forces. Since 2010 Djibouti has hosted the first Japanese overseas military base to be established since 1945 and frequently hosts vessels from other European and Asian navies."[166] In the same light as Djibouti, the KTO has ports in Busan and an air base in Osan that act as central ports of embarkation and debarkation. These nodes act as indispensable hubs for combined joint exercises such as Ulchi Freedom Guardian and Key Resolve, both annual exercises that strengthen the partnership of participating countries.

As the expansion of Djibouti acted as a regional logistics hub that brought with it significant inward investment from Gulf Arab states, regional logistics hubs in the KTO offer the same. Over time, the KTO expands to Pyongyang after stability operations and travels north. Sustainment planners consider the prospect of developing ports north of the DMZ to promote economic increase and regional stability. An example of prospective port improvement during the final phases of post-conflict reconstruction is the port of Nampo.

Djibouti strengthened its role as a conduit for African–Arab trade links, most notably for Dubai-based and Somali entrepreneurs, including those of southeast Ethiopia."[167] As in the case of Djibouti, the development of ports in North Korea is essential to achieving economic prosperity for the unified Korea that enables sustainment planners to extend operational reach and achieve U.S. national and strategic objectives.

The access to these ports will facilitate any residual humanitarian aid efforts for North Korea's 27 million inhabitants.

The daily requirements of the three million IDPs are nine million meals per day, 2.721 million gallons of bulk potable water per day, 30.06 million gallons of packaged water per day, and 570,000 pounds of medical supplies per day. The U.S. military has a shortfall that other actors can alleviate such as the ROK, UNC, CFC, and North Korea's infrastructure. The U.S. military will have a shortfall of, in total, 142 transportation medium truck cargo companies (40-Ton) for food, bulk potable and packaged water, and medical supplies.

In response to the Horn of Africa drought and subsequent famine in the summer of 2011, for example, U.S. emergency food aid programs provided $740 million to Ethiopia, Kenya, Somalia, South Sudan and Sudan (according to the U.S. State Department). It is fully consistent with American values to continue to respond vigorously and generously to emergencies in the region."[168] North Korean regime collapse will induce a yearly commitment in the same vignette as the Horn of Africa. Sustainment planners have the responsibility to support organizations committed to stability as North Korea's stability eliminates the prospect of organizations to fund terrorist activity."[169]

"The CJTF-HOA sustainment planner serves as the lead staff element for logistics planning in support of at least nine forward operating locations (FOLs) and for implementing processes to streamline the sustainment pipeline." The lead sustainment planners for USFK, EUSA, U.S. Army Pacific, USPACOM, and other agencies and organizations integrates multifunctional sustainment operation for the combined joint operating area. As in USAFRICOM and CJTF-HOA, the chief sustainment planner develops interoperable logistics concepts and doctrine and clearly identifies and integrates the appropriate logistics processes, organizations, and command and control options to meet the commander's intent in the joint environment."[170]

"In an effort to help its African partners cultivate their resources and further develop an organic African business infrastructure, USAFRICOM developed the Adaptive Logistics Network initiative."[171] In essence, North Korean regime collapse can ensure that there is also a repository of resident knowledge about the core capabilities of companies that can be accessed online to help avoid redundancy. To apply knowledge management, a central database can document credible KTO businesses and their capabilities with the intent of linking them with customers that include the U.S. military, nongovernmental organizations, contractors, and multinational corporations

In the 2010 Haiti earthquake, a primary means of delivery was through the Port-au-Prince seaport. The earthquake rendered both northern and southern piers unusable. North Korean seaports or airports may become unusable because of North Korean army attacks or derailment. Joint Task Force-Haiti, with assets from U.S. Transportation Command supported by the Army and Navy, initially established a Joint Logistics Over-the-Shore capability to bring supplies in from the sea. The sustainment planners must exercise this capability as the KTO planners conduct these exercises in Ulchi Freedom Guardian and Key Resolve each year. Non-combatant evacuation operations are also a sustainment planner's responsibility as Joint Logistics over the Shore in Haiti doubled the number of shipping containers received compared to pre-quake numbers.[172]

USSOUTHCOM established the JTF port opening element to repair the damaged southern pier and establish a temporary port capability. The KTO planners consistently tracks these events through the joint logistics operations center. Because of the massive scope of three million DPRK refugees, as learned in the 2010 Haiti earthquake, "U.S. military resources began arriving within days. On day one, two military planes began the distribution of essential food and water. Three thousand United States Army soldiers of the 82nd Airborne Division (Global Response Force) from Fort Bragg were sent in to establish a base to distribute food and water."[173] Additionally, the U.S. Air Force sent in 6,000 airmen and the U.S. Navy mustered 33 ships. U.S. Navy hospital ships arrived with salvage ships; U.S. Coast Guard buoy tenders attempted to re-open ports; U.S. Marines of the 22nd and 24th Marine Expeditionary Unit arrived with helicopter squadrons.[174]

The KTO's North Korean regime collapse can expect similar flow of forces that transportation planners integrate in receiving forces. As first responders in Haiti, the international community's delivery of emergency aid depended entirely on logistical support from the U.S. military."[175] Although the U.S. military is not the responsible agent for humanitarian aid, U.S. national leaders deploy the U.S. military because of its expeditionary and modular nature. The U.S. and coalition response to Haiti's earthquake lacked a designated JTF or joint logistics element . . . by a USSOUTHCOM staff with little force deployment planning capacity."[176]

The headquarters in USFK greatly mitigates this potential friction but two joint task forces may greater alleviate the two assumptions. One JTF can dedicate to the offensive operation whereas another JTF can dedicate to the refugee assistance. From its onset, JTF-H exercised command and control over military assets in support of the head agency, USAID, and a range of NGOs and the Government of Haiti to provide emergency disaster relief.[177]

The disarmament of North Korea is critical in fostering sustainability as the ROK military assumes broader nation-building efforts, but the ROK would require significant support from the international community to execute disarmament of North Korea.[178] Unlike the USEUCOM area of operations, an organization similar to NATO does not exist in and around the KTO to streamline diplomatic or military processes. During North Korean regime collapse, the Six Party Talks could effectively act as the beginning of a more structured multilateral agreement treaty in the USPACOM area of operations.[179] The total cost of reunification projects upwards of $200 billion.[180]

Humanitarian aid logistics involving North Korean regime collapse invites the management of supply chains in IDP management. Organizations such as the World Food Programme and International Federation of Red Cross and Red Crescent Societies conclude that humanitarian logistics are crucial to performance and serves as a bridge between disaster response and distribution with the military.[181] A successful sustainment operation is the key to defining success or failure in North Korean regime collapse. The U.S. military has the right command structure to command and control the sustainment architecture and shortfalls in commodities. USFK and PACOM are equipped with senior sustainment planners to implement the military concepts of agility, reservists, and pre-positioning for the management of sustainment required to support North Korean regime collapse.[182]

The U.S. military has the right industrial base to support deployment and force projection with organizations such as U.S. Transportation Command, Air Mobility Airlift

116

Command, Surface Deployment and Distribution Command, and Military Sealift

Command. Despite the convoluted nature of the different types of money spent on

different funding categories, the U.S. military experiences success in projecting the force.

So long as the U.S. military provides the security for NGOs, such as Cooperative for

Assistance and Relief Everywhere, to work in dangerous situations, the solution to an

insecure environment is to provision humanitarian aid from the core responsibility of

security.[183]

---

[1]Ian Oliver, *War and Peace in the Balkans: The Diplomacy of Conflict in the Former Yugoslavia* (London: Tauris, 2005), 6.

[2]Ibid.

[3]Ibid., 7.

[4]Ibid.

[5]Ibid.

[6]Landon E. Hancock and C R. Mitchell, eds., *Zones of Peace* (Bloomfield, CT: Kumarian Press, 2007), 123.

[7]Ibid., 125.

[8]Ibid.

[9]Ibid.

[10]Ibid., 126.

[11]Ibid.

[12]Evelyn N. Farkas, *Fractured States and U.S. Foreign Policy: Iraq, Ethiopia, and Bosnia in the 1990s* (New York: Palgrave Macmillan, 2003), 76.

[13]Ibid.

[14]Derek H. Chollet, *The Road to the Dayton Accords: A Study of American Statecraft* (New York: Palgrave Macmillan, 2005), 183.

[15] Ibid., 200.

[16] Farkas, *Fractured States and U.S. Foreign Policy*, 71.

[17] Ibid., 80.

[18] Ibid.

[19] Ibid., 78.

[20] Ibid., 79.

[21] Ibid.

[22] Ibid.

[23] Ibid, 82.

[24] Ibid., 83.

[25] Larry Minear, *The Humanitarian Enterprise: Dilemmas and Discoveries* (Bloomfield, CT: Kumarian Press, 2002), 45.

[26] Ibid.

[27] Minear, *The Humanitarian Enterprise*, 171.

[28] Ibid.

[29] Ibid., 185-186.

[30] Ibid.

[31] Ibid., 215.

[32] Badredine Arfi, *International Change and the Stability of Multiethnic States: Yugoslavia, Lebanon, and Crises of Governance* (Bloomington: Indiana University Press, 2005), 113.

[33] Ibid.

[34] Farkas, *Fractured States and U.S. Foreign Policy,* 77.

[35] Ibid.

[36] Ibid.

[37]Ibid.

[38]Ibid.

[39]Ibid., 78.

[40]Ibid., 116.

[41]Daniel Byman and Kenneth M. Pollack, *Things Fall Apart: Containing the Spillover from an Iraqi Civil War* (Washington, DC: Brookings Institution Press, 2007), 189.

[42]Council of Europe Commissioner for Human Rights, *Post-War Justice and Durable Peace in the Former Yugoslavia: Issue Paper* (France: Council of Europe Publishing, 2012), 12.

[43]Minear, *The Humanitarian Enterprise,* 85.

[44]Ibid., 216.

[45]Roberta Arnold, ed., *Law Enforcement Within the Framework of Peace Support Operations*, International and Comparative Criminal Law Series (Leiden: Martinus Nijhoff Publishers, 2008), 140.

[46]Ibid., 146.

[47]Ibid., 154.

[48]Ibid., 147.

[49]Willie C. Jordan, "Logistics Challenges in Support of Operations in Bosnia (OOTW)" (Strategy Research Project, U.S. Army War College, Carlisle Barracks, PA, June 5, 2001), 1.

[50]United States Army Europe (USAREUR), AE Pamphlet 525-100, *Military Operations: the U.S. Army in Bosnia and Herzegovina* (Heidelberg, Germany: U.S. Army Europe and Seventh Army, October 7, 2003), 21.

[51]Ibid., 18.

[52]Shawn P. Walsh, "Bulk Fuel Support in Bosnia," *Army Logistician* 31, no. 4 (July/August 1999): 4, http://www.alu.army.mil/alog/issues/JulAug99/MS436.htm (accessed May 13, 2014).

[53]Ibid.

[54]Ibid.

[55]Larry K. Wentz, *Lessons from Bosnia: The IFOR Experience* (Honolulu, Hawaii: University Press of the Pacific, 2002), xi.

[56]Ibid.

[57]Ibid., 31.

[58]Ibid., 50.

[59]Robert I. Rotberg, *Battling Terrorism in the Horn of Africa* (Cambridge, MA: World Peace Foundation, 2005), 94.

[60]Gaim Kibreab, *Eritrea: A Dream Deferred*, Eastern Africa Series (Oxford: James Currey, 2009), 402.

[61]Rotberg, *Battling Terrorism in the Horn of Africa*, 65.

[62]Kibreab, *Eritrea: A Dream Deferred*, 402.

[63]Iyob, *The Eritrean Struggle for Independence*, 124.

[64]Ibid., 123.

[65]Rotberg, *Battling Terrorism in the Horn of Africa*, 65.

[66]Ibid., 100.

[67]Ibid., 94.

[68]Ibid.

[69]Lata, "The Ethiopia-Eritrea War," 384.

[70]Ibid.

[71]Rotberg, *Battling Terrorism in the Horn of Africa*, 101.

[72]Ibid.

[73]Ibid.

[74]Ibid.

[75]Peter Woodward, *US Foreign Policy and the Horn of Africa* (Aldershot, Hants, England: Ashgate Publishing, 2006), 88.

[76]Ibid.

[77]Ibid.

[78]Ibid.

[79]Rotberg, *Battling Terrorism in the Horn of Africa*, 69.

[80]Ibid.

[81]Ibid.

[82]Ibid.

[83]Ibid.

[84]Ibid., 70.

[85]Ibid.

[86]Ibid., 87.

[87]Ibid.

[88]Ibid., 102.

[89]Ibid.

[90]Woodward, *US Foreign Policy and the Horn of Africa*, 85.

[91]Ibid.

[92]Ibid.

[93]Ibid.

[94]Rotberg, *Battling Terrorism in the Horn of Africa*, 111.

[95]Ibid.

[96]Ibid.

[97]Ibid.

[98]Ibid., 20.

[99]Ibid., 108.

[100]Ibid., 111.

[101]Global Humanitarian Assistance. "Country Profile: Ethiopia." http://www. globalhumanitarianassistance.org/countryprofile/ethiopia (accessed May 4, 2014).

[102]Paul Henze, *Ethiopia Analysis and Text of a Soviet Report: Crisis of a Marxist Economy* (Santa Monica, CA: Rand, April 1989), A-24.

[103]Rotberg, *Battling Terrorism in the Horn of Africa*, 94.

[104]Ibid.

[105]Ibid., 95.

[106]Ibid., 108.

[107]Woodward, *US Foreign Policy and the Horn of Africa*, 82.

[108]Redie Bereketeab, *State-Building in Post Liberation Eritrea: Challenges, Achievements and Potentials* (London: Adonis and Abbey Publishers, 2009), 170.

[109]Ibid., 171.

[110]Ibid., 196.

[111]Ibid.

[112]Ibid., 81.

[113]Woodward, *US Foreign Policy and the Horn of Africa*, 80.

[114]Ibid.

[115]Daniel Volman, *Obama, AFRICOM, and U.S. Military Policy Toward Africa: Working Paper Number 14* (Evanston, IL: Daniel Volman, 2009), 3.

[116]Dan Henk, *Uncharted Paths, Uncertain Vision: U.S. Military Involvements in Sub-Saharan Africa in the Wake of the Cold War* (Colorado: USAF Institute for National Security Studies, 1998), 19.

[117]Ibid., 43.

[118]Stephen Burgess, *Has the US Military in the Horn of Africa Been a Force That Embraces Strategic Knowledge and Perspective in Countering Violent Extremism and Assisting with Sustainable Development?* (Maxwell Air Force Base: US Air War College, 2013), 7.

[119]Ibid., 9.

[120]The White House, *U.S. Strategy toward Sub-Saharan Africa* (Washington, DC: The White House, June 2012), 6.

[121]David Styan, *Djibouti: Changing Influence in the Horn's Strategic Hub*: *Chatham House Briefing Papers* (London: Chatham House, April 2013): 4.

[122]Mark Schuller and Pablo Morales, *Tectonic Shifts: Haiti Since the Earthquake* (Sterling, VA: Kumarian Press, 2012), 1.

[123]Ibid.

[124]Ibid.

[125]Ibid., 2.

[126]Ibid., 30.

[127]Jorge Heine and Andrew S. Thompson, eds., *Fixing Haiti: MINUSTAH and Beyond* (New York: United Nations University Press, 2011), 230.

[128]Ibid.

[129]USSOUTHCOM, "Operation Unified Response: Support to Haiti Earthquake Relief 2010" http://www.southcom.mil/newsroom/Pages/Operation-Unified-Response-Support-to-Haiti-Earthquake-Relief-2010.aspx (accessed May 4, 2014).

[130]Ibid.

[131]Schuller and Morales, *Tectonic Shifts*, 218.

[132]Ibid.

[133]Ibid.

[134]Ibid., 220.

[135]Jorge Heine and Andrew S. Thompson, eds., *Fixing Haiti: MINUSTAH and Beyond* (New York: United Nations University Press, 2011), 187.

[136]Ibid., 234.

[137]Ibid., 236.

[138]Ibid.

[139]Ibid., 242.

[140]Schuller and Morales, *Tectonic* Shifts, 30.

[141]Ibid.

[142]Ibid., 218.

[143]Ibid., 77.

[144]Ibid.

[145]Ibid., 82.

[146]Ibid., 31.

[147]Ibid., 195.

[148]Ibid., 199.

[149]Ibid.

[150]Ibid., 202.

[151]Ken Keen et al., "Foreign Disaster Response: Joint Task Force-Haiti Observations," *Military Review* (November-December 2010): 85.

[152]U.S. Southern Command, *Operation Unified Response: First 100 Days (January 13-April 23, 2010)* (Miami, FL: U.S. Southern Command Fact Sheet, April 23, 2010), 1.

[153]Ibid.

[154]Ibid., 86.

[155]Ibid., 86-87.

[156]Wentz, *Lessons from Bosnia: The IFOR Experience*, 51.

[157]Ibid., 102.

[158]Ibid., 147.

[159]Ibid., 332.

[160]Ibid., 371.

[161]Steven Bowman, *Bosnia: U.S. Military Operations: CRS Issue Brief for Congress, Order Code IB93056* (Washington, DC: Congressional Research Service: The Library of Congress, 2003), 1.

[162]United States Army Europe (USAREUR), *Military Operations: the U.S. Army in Bosnia and Herzegovina,* 14.

[163]Ibid., 25.

[164]Harold Raugh Jr., *Operation Joint Endeavor: V Corps in Bosnia-Herzegovina 1995-1996, an Oral History* (Fort Leavenworth, KS: Combat Studies Institute Press; US Army Combined Arms Center, 2010), 15-16.

[165]Ibid., 85.

[166]Styan, *Djibouti: Changing Influence in the Horn's Strategic Hub*, 4.

[167]Ibid., 17.

[168]John Banks et al., *Top Five Reasons Why Africa Should Be a Priority for the United States: Africa Growth Initiative at Brookings* (Washington, DC: Brookings Institute, March 2013): 14.

[169]Ibid., 15.

[170]Akil King, Zackary Moss, and Afi Pittman, "Overcoming Logistics Challenges in East Africa," *Army Sustainment* (January-February 2014): 30.

[171]Ibid., 31.

[172]Keen et al., "Foreign Disaster Response: Joint Task Force-Haiti Observations," 88.

[173]David DiOrio, "Operation Unified Response – Haiti Earthquake 2010," *Unified Response* (November 2010): 2.

[174]Ibid.

[175]Ibid., 6.

[176]Ibid., 8.

[177]Keen et al., "Foreign Disaster Response: Joint Task Force-Haiti Observations, 85.

[178]The Asia Foundation, *North Korea Contingency Planning and U.S.-ROK Cooperation* (Washington, DC: Center for U.S.-Korea Policy, September 2009).

[179]Ibid.

[180]Charles Wolf, *Straddling Economics and Politics: Cross-Cutting Issues in Asia, the United States, and the Global Economy* (Santa Monica, CA: Rand, 2002), 204, http://www.rand.org/publications/mr/mr1571/ (accessed May 5, 2014).

[181]L. N. Wassenhove, "Humanitarian Aid Logistics: Supply Chain Management in High Gear," *The Journal of the Operational Research Society* 57, no. 5 (May 2006): 475.

[182]Dawn Russell and John Saldanha, "Five Tenets of Security-Aware Logistics and Supply Chain Operation, *Transportation Journal* 42, no. 4 (Summer 2003): 44-54.

[183]Sarah Lischer, "Military Intervention and the Humanitarian 'Force Multiplier'," *Global Governance* 13, no. 1 (January-March 2007): 99-118.

CHAPTER 5

CONCLUSIONS AND RECOMMENDATIONS

An analysis of the forecasted North Korean regime collapse against the three case studies of Yugoslavia, Ethiopia, and Haiti by applying the ETM shows a niche role for sustainment planners to coordinate across all Joint, Interagency, Intergovernmental, and Multinational (JIIM) actors to leverage the shortfalls of over 40 truck companies. This study will make a few recommendations on how United States military sustainment planners can prepare for North Korean regime collapse with an appreciation of the magnitude of requirements ranging from over 11,000,000 meals a day to millions of gallons of fuel. Those preparations will take the form of training United States military, ROK, interagency, multinational, and other strategic sustainment planners and anticipating preparations and relationships for North Korean regime collapse.

Sustaining North Korean Regime Collapse:
Whole-of-Government Approach

Sustainment and sustainment units require several tasks to facilitate a realistic plan to support the organic offensive operation and three million IDPs. As evidenced in the support of an offensive operation, the U.S. military has enough organic capability, given the commodity stocks to support the fight (ammunition, fuel, water, etc) for a brigade combat team. Each brigade combat team owns a support battalion; there is no shortfall when supporting the offensive operation. The challenge in planning successful sustainment to achieve U.S. national objectives is to conduct planning, training, and preparations to ensure the United States government prepares itself for the North Korean regime collapse humanitarian crisis.

Sustainment planners need to ensure the theater specific plans consider the magnitude of the shortfalls and the lessons learned from Yugoslavia, Haiti, and Ethiopia. The U.S. response in Yugoslavia was adequate that led to stability in the region today. The U.S. response in Ethiopia was somewhat limited and was a failure in diplomacy. Haiti was an example where the U.S. military provided relief supplies to the millions of IDPs. By comparing the number of expected IDPs, in this case three million, the standard consumption ratios set by the default in *Operational Logistics Planner software* can help determine the time and space requirements and the types and amount of units to sustain North Korean regime collapse.

Because of the numerous shortfalls outlined in this manuscript of existing assets in the KTO, many of the other sustainment tasks fall outside of U.S. military competence. The application and synchronization of interagency support to solve the issue is solvable through actions by other organizations (NGO/IGO, other U.S. departments, allied nations) in the absence of civil capabilities and then only until other more appropriate organizations can take charge of such efforts. The whole-of-government approach is essential and relevant to a period of constrained resources.

Clearly, North Korean regime collapse is not solely a U.S. military problem. As the first responder, the U.S. military can set the parameters for success as in the case of Yugoslavia and Haiti. Over time, IGOs, NGOs, and other allied nations can surge effects that positively influence outcomes that nest with U.S. policies. Other actors alleviate and lessen the burden of sustainment from the U.S. military. A requirement to avoid the U.S. military failing in long-term sustainment is for other state and non-state actors to involve themselves in delivering supplies, improving infrastructure, facilitating elections, establishing new ports, analyzing new imports and exports, and sustaining new economic sanctions. Sustainment planners must become agile during yearly exercises of Ulchi Freedom Guardian, Key Resolve, and Foal Eagle to plan for North Korean regime collapse. Military sustainment planners must also integrate host-nation support with the ROK.

Findings and Recommendations: JIIM Integration
and Unity of Effort

Comparing the case studies, the U.S. national posture on the KTO greatly improves the capability to respond to North Korean regime collapse. To address the thesis assertion, the primary emphasis of how the U.S. military conduct sustainment during a North Korean regime collapse is to ensure a common U.S. strategy rather than a collection of individual departmental and agency efforts and on mobilizing and involving all available U.S. government assets in the effort. An early and often-communicated policy on the KTO can alleviate most of the consternation of a sustainment planner.

The existing force structure on the KTO is limited and will have shortfalls. The numbers required to sustain a brigade combat team against a NK threat is substantial, but sustainable because of the organic assets in each brigade combat team that will deploy to the KTO in response to the DPRK military's efforts to combat south of the DMZ. The real challenge lies in the shortfalls of distribution capabilities because of the finite number of truck companies for three million refugees. LOGCAP, as in the case of Yugoslavia, can help alleviate the burden and satisfy requirements. NGOs can also provide the same type of assistance.

Other services on the KTO include the U.S. Air Force, U.S. Navy, U.S. Marine

Corps, and Special Operations Forces. The U.S. Air Force has 7th U.S. Air Force in Osan

Air Base with roughly 8,000 airmen. The U.S. Navy has 300 sailors and the U.S. Marine

Corps has 100 Marines in Korea. Special Operations Forces accumulate to roughly 100

members. The other services, with the exception of the U.S. Army likely will not have

the immediate means to partake in humanitarian relief missions.

The U.S. military will have a shortfall of at least 15 transportation medium truck

cargo companies (40-Ton) truck companies for food, 12 transportation medium truck

cargo companies (40-Ton) for bulk potable, 114 transportation medium truck cargo

companies (40-Ton) for and packaged water, and one transportation medium truck cargo

companies (40-Ton) for medical supplies. The U.S. military will be able to support a

small fraction of these requirements of shortfall forecasts are over 120,775 short tons of

commodities (meals, packaged water, and medical supplies), 2.721 million gallons of

water, and 386,808 gallons of fuel to support the 142 total transportation medium truck

cargo companies (40-Ton). Of the different types of available non-divisional companies,

any number of permutations to create a task organization for 3 million IDPs ultimately

prove limited. The U.S. military will absorb the initial mission because they are the first

responders. Over time, the U.S. military will culminate early if the ROK does not have a

sufficient plan in place to distribute and store commodities.

Other options that military sustainment planners explore are the use of boxcar

railheads. The ROK has a modern infrastructure and the DPRK has a network of

thousands of miles of track. The cubic feet for a 60-foot standard boxcar is 6,085 feet.

One cubic feet of rations holds 12 meals. Multiplying both values, a military sustainment planner can conclude that each boxcar can hold 73,020 meals. To meet the distribution rail capability for 9 million meals needed to sustain 3 million IDPs, 124 boxcars are sufficient. A solid rail system can alleviate the pressure of the U.S. military supplying food, water, and medical supplies along paved roads in an unwieldy security situation.

The U.S. military has a shortfall that other actors can alleviate such as the ROK, UNC, CFC, and North Korea's infrastructure. The shortfall of 142 transportation medium truck cargo companies (40-Ton) the military requires transporting goods and services for water, subsistence, fuel, and medical supplies three million IDPs is staggering. To mitigate shortfalls, multinational cooperation, especially with the ROK, is essential. The ROK must take the majority of the responsibility during North Korean regime collapse. Of the 142 transportation medium truck cargo companies (40-Ton) required, the U.S. military can reasonably support a potential of 5 to 10 percent by deploying several transportation companies. The host-nation support assets are key to closing the gap of the other 90 percent of required distribution capabilities.

This alleviates the burden of distribution that the ROK can cover in the best interests of the U.S. North Korean regime collapse will require heavy interagency support to gain leverage and win the confidence of the North Korean constituents. The challenge is to coordinate for LOGCAP services, leveraging ROK assets through sustained partnership, NGO/IGO support, USAID involvement, USPACOM JIACG coordination, and synchronization of the whole-of-government approach to ensure three million IDPs meet required sustenance to favor the American presence.

Sustainment planners need to provide transparency for all the logistics, personnel services, and health services support data gathered from the entire JIIM environment in the KTO. Sustainment planners need to translate sustainment intelligence into terms that make sense for commanders to make the decisions required to achieve national objectives. The principles of war and the principles of joint/multinational sustainment are a start to achieving the common language required for a base understanding of the shortfalls and achieving momentum. Sustainment planners need to expose all layered geospatial information and the consumption data open to the JIIM environment and welcome interworking relationships with unanticipated partners. Unity of effort is critical to achieving desired effects.

Scenarios in the yearly training exercises should inculcate and challenge sustainment planners with the fidelity in supporting three million IDPs in unimproved terrain. Sustainment planners require to facilitate the buildup of IDP sites, plans to secure commodity stocks, building sustainment common operating pictures to support the stability operation, training for North Korean regime collapse with partners, and building key relationships with the JIIM community. Successful integration of all key JIIM actors includes leveling the playing field with common language and terms, early planning, and proficiency in cross-pollination of sustainment tasks.

The new ROK President Park Geun-hye, effective February 2013, pursued a principled policy that conditions economic benefits to provide North Korea meaningful change.[1] This policy indicates a requirement for the ROK to provide humanitarian assistance to North Korea while promoting economic and social benefits. The level of emergency food aid can be determined in the JIIM environment through international aid organizations albeit the U.S. and ROK military, through partnership, are the first responders to such crises. A key component is to deliver directly the supplies to the needy rather than provision the relief supplies to legacy North Korean leadership post-regime collapse. Concurrently, the ROK should think of leveraging its alliance cooperation and bilateral agreements with the U.S. and other allies to bolster the ROK's off-peninsula contributions to project global influence in the international community, enhancing its profile and credibility.[2]

The United States must have the capabilities to increase the governance capacities of weak states and not ignore that the reconstruction of North Korea involves reunification that will also impact Korea's economy. Although the U.S. pronounced a pivot to the Asia-Pacific, budgetary constraints limit the amount of resources implemented in the KTO for sustainment planners to use. The only way to successfully monitor and achieve the strategic end state is the collective involvement of all the available resources of the U.S. government (military and civilian), nongovernmental organizations (NGOs), and international partners. Although military assets are an essential component of many post-conflict reconstruction operations such as a NK regime collapse, specific military goals and objectives are only a portion of the larger operation. The imperative is for sustainment planners relentlessly to observe actions on the KTO because Kim Jung Un is clear that North Korea will not relinquish its nuclear weapons capabilities at any price.[3]

Areas for Further Research

This study did not directly consider the People's Republic of China's response to a North Korean regime collapse. Practitioners profess the theory that China continues to aid North Korea to prevent more refugees from crossing the border into China. Despite being a signatory to the 1951 UN Convention Relating to the Status of Refugees, China does not acknowledge North Koreans as refugees but as economic migrants.[4] A future area for further research could attempt to solve a baseline reaction of China and its inherent sustainment implications as North Korea maintains closer ties with China than with any other country.[5] Other practitioners can use the ETM for other case studies such as Operation Iraqi Freedom, Operation Enduring Freedom, the Japan Tsunami disaster, or the many other historical vignettes in U.S. military history to apply to North Korean regime collapse.

Instead of the ETM, future studies can incorporate other JIIM information management matrices such as Political-Military-Economic-Social-Information-Infrastructure-Physical Environment-Time analysis, Areas-Structures-Capabilities-Organizations-People-Events assessment, and Sewage-Water-Electricity-Academics-Trash-Medical-Unemployment-Security considerations. Other areas to suggest for further research are to list all the JIIM actors in North Korean regime collapse. Other efforts may include the effects and calculations affecting the terrain and unimproved infrastructure in North Korea on sustainment capability and operational readiness rates of military equipment. These attempts to analyze data would benefit sustainment planning in North Korean regime collapse.

Closing Remarks

This was an individual research project based on assumptions (offensive operation coupled with humanitarian aid) that are not foreign to the history of U.S. conflicts, as reflected in the case studies of Yugoslavia, Ethiopia, and Haiti. The case studies and the analysis reflect that if U.S. undermines a conflict or significant regime change, regional instability leads to threats against the U.S.

134

The probability of terrorists, transnational crime organizations, or violent extremist organizations harboring refuge in failed post-conflict reconstruction projects increases. Therefore, the researcher believes that the findings and recommendations of this research could facilitate as a basis of research and inquiry for individuals interested in conducting future assertions on regime collapse. The model used in this thesis can apply to potential regime collapse throughout the world with application of the ETM model, consumption factors dependent on new information and situations, and capabilities to provide sustainment.

To close, each analysis of regime collapse is unique to the given researcher and regional study. However, the key highlight to identify success or failure of sustainment in regime collapse is the successful synchronization and integration of the JIIM environment. In this regard, indeed, North Korean regime collapse has the potential to be a resounding and comparative success with application to the lessons learned in the aforementioned case studies. The ability to sustain a post-regime collapse reconstruction effort is critical to the security of the U.S., her allies, and democratic ideals.

---

[1]Bruce Klinger, "The U.S. Should Support New South Korean President's Approach to North Korea," *Backgrounder* 2789 (April 11, 2013): 1.

[2]Scott Snyder, *Strengthening the U.S.-ROK Alliance* (Center for U.S.-Korea Policy: The Asia Foundation, February 2009), 14.

[3]Hong Yung Lee, "North Korea in 2012: Kim Jong Un's Succession," *Asian Survey* 53, no. 1 (January/February 2013): 176-83.

[4]Balbina Y. Hwang, *Furthering North Korean Human Rights Through U.S.-ROK Cooperation* (Washington, DC: Center for U.S.-Korea Policy: The Asia Foundation, April 2011), 8.

[5]Bernd Schaefer, *Overconfidence Shattered: North Korean Unification Policy, 1971-1975* (Washington, DC: North Korea International Documentation Project: Woodrow Wilson International Center for Scholars, December 2010), 3.

APPENDIX A

BENEFITS OF KOREA UNIFICATION

Table 9.   Benefits of Korean Unification

Photo Removed Due to Copyright Restrictions

Source: Huh Moon Young, *Basic Reading On Korean Unification* (Seoul, Republic of Korea: Korea Institute for National Unification (KINU), 2012), 10.

APPENDIX B

SUMMARY OF CONFLICTS IN NORTHEAST ASIA

Figure 12. Conflicts in Northeast Asia.

Source: Huh Moon Young, *Basic Reading On Korean Unification* (Seoul, Republic of Korea: Korea Institute for National Unification (KINU), 2012), 104.

APPENDIX C

NORTH KOREA'S SURVIVAL STRATEGY

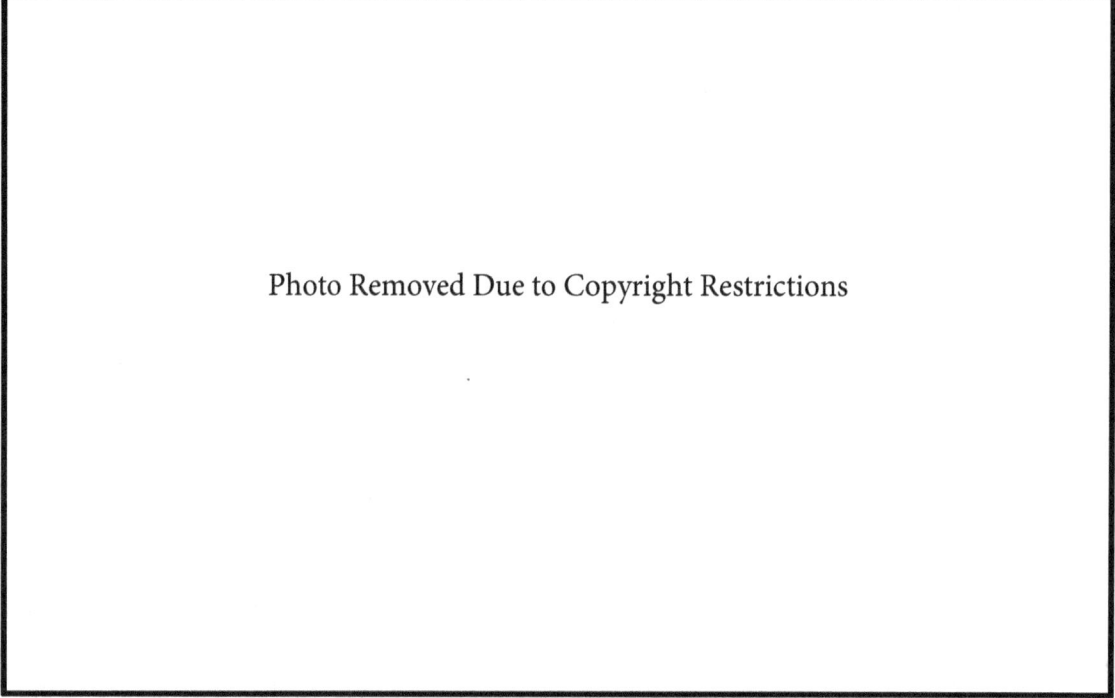

Figure 13. The Structure of North Korea's Survival Strategy

Source: Huh Moon Young, *Basic Reading On Korean Unification* (Seoul, Republic of Korea: Korea Institute for National Unification (KINU), 2012), 167.

APPENDIX D

YONGBYON NUCLEAR CENTER

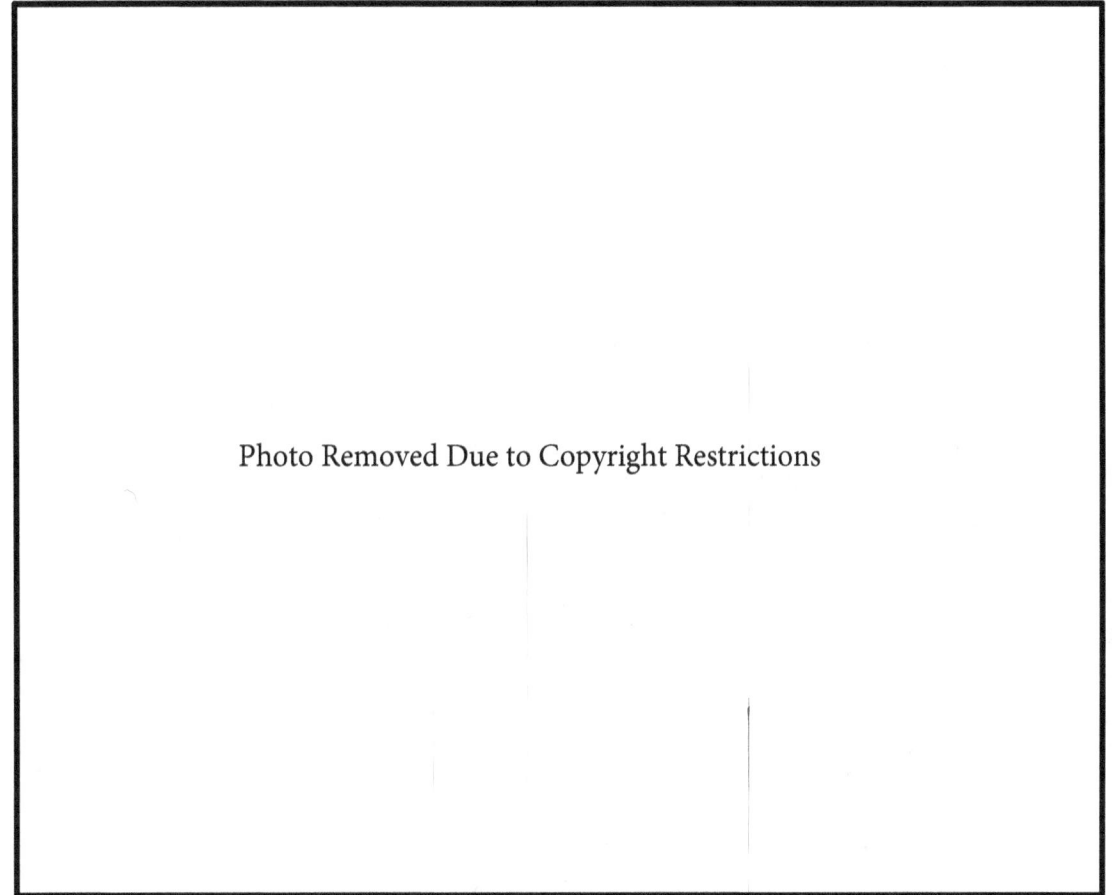

Figure 14. Commercial Satellite Image From March 8, 2011 for the 5 Megawatt Reactor
At The Yongbyon Nuclear Center

Source: Institute for Science and International Security, "Isis Reports: New Satellite
Image of Construction at North Korea Nuclear Site," Institute for Science and
International Security, http://isis-online.org/isis-reports/detail/new-satellite-image-of-
construction-at-north-korea-nuclear-site/10 (accessed May 5, 2014).

APPENDIX E

KOREA THEATER OF OPERATIONS

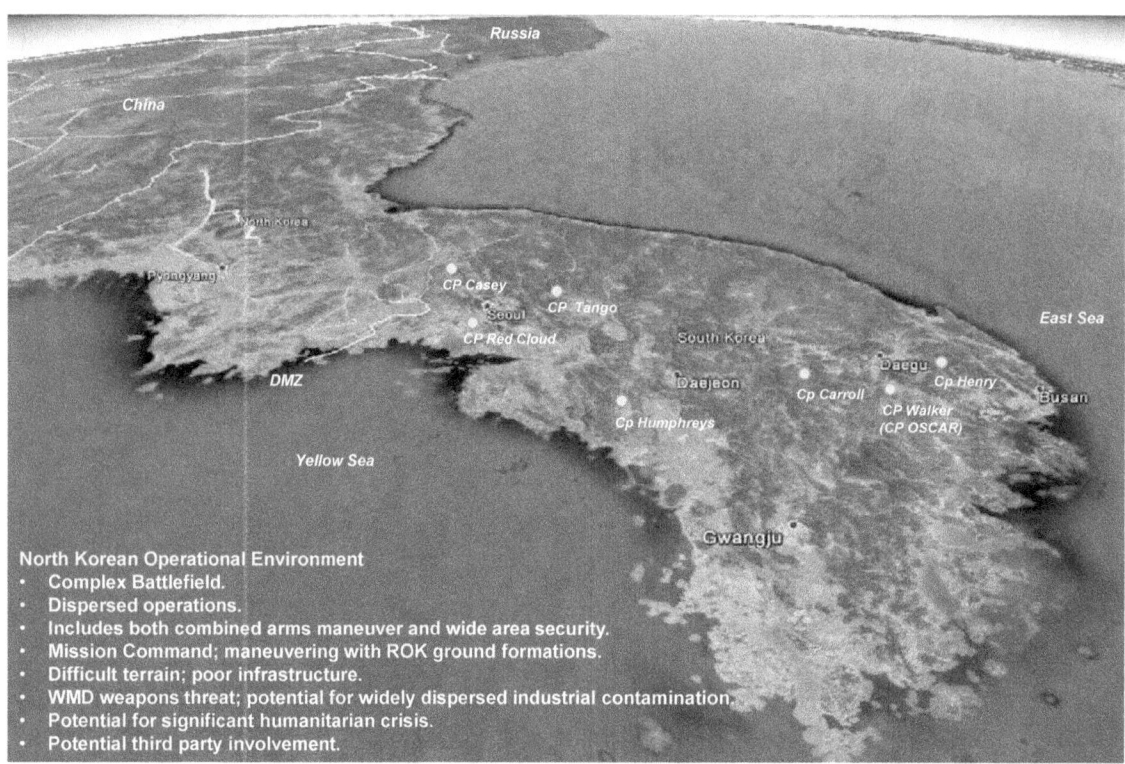

Figure 15. U.S. Military: Korea Theater of Operations and North Korean Operational Environment Considerations

Source: Created by author.

BIBLIOGRAPHY

Arfi, Badredine. *International Change and the Stability of Multiethnic States: Yugoslavia, Lebanon, and Crises of Governance*. Bloomington: Indiana University Press, 2005.

Arnold, Roberta, ed. *Law Enforcement within the Framework of Peace Support Operations*. International and Comparative Criminal Law Series. Leiden: Martinus Nijhoff Publishers, 2008.

Banks, John, George Ingram, Mwangi Kimenyi, Steven Rocker, Witney Schneidman, Yun Sun, and Lesley Anne Warner. "Top Five Reasons Why Africa Should Be a Priority for the United States." *Africa Growth Initiative at Brookings* (March 2013).

Barton, Frederick, and Bathsheba Crocker. *Progress or Peril? Measuring Iraq's Reconstruction: The Post-Conflict Reconstruction Project*. Washington, DC: Center for Strategic and International Studies, 2004.

BBC News, *North Korea's Missile Programme*. April 12, 2013. http://www.bbc.co.uk/news/world-asia-17399847 (accessed February 7, 2014).

Beck, Peter M. "North Korea in 2010." *Asian Survey* 51, no. 1 (February 2011): 33-40. http://dx.doi.org/10.1525/as.2011.51.1.33 (accessed October 17, 2013).

———. "North Korea in 2011." *Asian Survey* 52, no. 1 (February 2012): 52-64 http://dx.doi.org/10.1525/as.2012.52.1.65 (accessed October 17, 2013).

Beller, Sarah, Graig Klein, and Ronald Fisher. *Us Government Innovations in Peacebuilding and Conflict Resolution: Implications for the IPCR Program*. Washington, DC: School of International Service (SIS), American University, 2010.

Bennett, Bruce W. *Preparing for the Possibility of a North Korean Collapse*. Santa Monica, CA: Rand, 2013.

———. *Uncertainties in the North Korean Nuclear Threat*. Santa Monica, CA: Rand, 2010.

Bensahel, Nora. "Organising for Nation Building." *Survival* 49, no. 2 (June 2007): 43-76. http://dx.doi.org/10.1080/00396330701437827 (accessed April 28, 2014).

Bereketeab, Redie. *State-Building in Post Liberation Eritrea: Challenges, Achievements and Potentials*. London: Adonis and Abbey Publishers, 2009.

Bowman, Steven. *Bosnia: U.S. Military Operations: CRS Issue Brief for Congress, Order Code IB93056.* Washington, DC: Congressional Research Service: The Library of Congress, 2003.

Burgess, Stephen *Has the US Military in the Horn of Africa Been a Force That Embraces Strategic Knowledge and Perspective in Countering Violent Extremism and Assisting with Sustainable Development?* Maxwell Air Force Base: US Air War College, 2013.

Byman, Daniel, and Kenneth M. Pollack. *Things Fall Apart: Containing the Spillover from an Iraqi Civil War.* Washington, DC: Brookings Institution Press, 2007.

Cecchine, Gary, Forest Morgan, Michael Wermuth, Timothy Jackson, Agnes Schaefer, and Matthew Stafford. *The U.S. Military Response to the 2010 Haiti Earthquake: Considerations for Army Leaders.* Santa Monica, CA: Rand, 2013.

Central Intelligence Agency. "The World Factbook: North Korea." CIA World Factbook. https://www.cia.gov/library/publications/the-world-factbook/geos/kn.html (accessed May 1, 2014).

Chollet, Derek H. *The Road to the Dayton Accords: A Study of American Statecraft.* New York: Palgrave Macmillan, 2005.

Commissioner for Human Rights, Council of Europe. *Post-War Justice and Durable Peace in the Former Yugoslavia: Issue Paper.* France: Council of Europe Publishing, 2012.

Creswell, John W. *Qualitative Inquiry and Research Design: Choosing Among Five Approaches.* 3rd ed. Thousand Oaks: SAGE, 2012.

Cyril, Michael. *Operational Logistics.* Fort Leavenworth, KS: United States Army Command and General Staff College, 2001).

DiOrio, David. "Operation Unified Response–Haiti Earthquake 2010." *Unified Response* (November 2010).

Epstein, Jennifer. "Obama Warns North Korea." Politico, March 25, 2012. http://www.politico.com/news/stories/0312/74434.html#ixzz2jF5IMeET (accessed November 11, 2013).

Farkas, Evelyn N. *Fractured States and U.S. Foreign Policy: Iraq, Ethiopia, and Bosnia in the 1990s.* New York: Palgrave Macmillan, 2003.

Fehrenbach, T. R. *This Kind of War: The Classic Korean War History.* 50th ed. Washington, DC: Brassey, 2000.

Fitzpatrick, Mark. "Stopping Nuclear North Korea," *Survival* 51, no. 4 (September 2009): 5-12, http://dx.doi.org/10.1080/00396330903168782 (accessed October 17, 2013).

Ford, Glyn. "North Korea in Transition." *Soundings*, no. 43 (Winter 2009).

Global Humanitarian Assistance. "Country Profile: Ethiopia." http://www. globalhumanitarianassistance.org/countryprofile/ethiopia (accessed May 4, 2014).

Grey, Jeffrey. "The Korean War," *Journal of Contemporary History* 39, no. 4 (October 2004): 667-676. http://dx.doi.org/10.1177/0022009404046787 (accessed October 17, 2013).

Hagström, Linus, and Marie Soderberg, eds. *North Korea Policy: Japan and the Great Powers*. New York, NY: Routledge, 2006.

Hancock, Landon E., and C. R. Mitchell, eds. *Zones of Peace*. Bloomfield, CT: Kumarian Press, 2007.

Headquarters, Army Forces Far East, *Logistics Study of the Korean Campaigns: 1950-1953*. San Francisco, CA: Operations Research Office.

Heine, Jorge, and Andrew S. Thompson, eds. *Fixing Haiti: MINUSTAH and Beyond*. New York: United Nations University Press, 2011.

Heit, Shannon. "Waging sexual warfare: Case studies of rape warfare used by the Japanese Imperial Army during World War II." *Women's Studies International Forum* 32, no. 5 (September 2009): 363-70. http://dx.doi.org/10.1016/j.wsif.2009.07.010 (accessed April 28, 2014).

Henk, Dan. *Uncharted Paths, Uncertain Vision: U.S. Military Involvements in Sub-Saharan Africa in the Wake of the Cold War*. Colorado: USAF Institute for National Security Studies, 1998.

Henze, Paul. *Ethiopia Analysis and Text of a Soviet Report: Crisis of a Marxist Economy* Santa Monica, CA: Rand, April 1989:

Herren, Thomas. Briefing Conference on the Republic of Korea for Unified Command Mission to the ROK. Tokyo: General Headquarters, United Nations Command, 1952.

Hwang, Balbina. *Furthering North Korean Human Rights Through U.S.-ROK Cooperation*. Washington, DC: Center for U.S.-Korea Policy: The Asia Foundation, April 2011.

Institute for Science and International Security. "Isis Reports: New Satellite Image of Construction at North Korea Nuclear Site." Institute for Science and International

Security. http://isis-online.org/isis-reports/detail/new-satellite-image-of-construction-at-north-korea-nuclear-site/10 (accessed May 5, 2014).

Iyob, Ruth. *The Eritrean Struggle for Independence: Domination, Resistance, Nationalism, 1941-1993 (African Studies)*. Cambridge: Cambridge University Press, 1997.

Jordan, Willie C. *Logistics Challenges in Support of Operations in Bosnia (OOTW)*, Strategy Research Project. Carlisle Barracks, PA: U.S. Army War College, June 5, 2001.

Keen, Ken, Matthew Elledge, Charles Nolan, and Jennifer Kimmey. "Foreign Disaster Response: Joint Task Force-Haiti Observations." *Military Review* (November-December 2010): 85-96.

Kibreab, Gaim. *Eritrea: A Dream Deferred*. Eastern Africa Series. Oxford: James Currey, 2009.

Kim Hyun Sik. "The Secret History Of Kim Jong Il." *Foreign Policy*, no. 168 (September 2008): 44-53. http://search.proquest.com/docview/224037546?accountid=458.

Kim, Samuel, and Tai Hwan Lee. *North Korea and Northeast Asia.* Lanham, MD: Rowman and Littlefield Publishers, 2002.

King, Akil, Zackary Moss, and Afi Pittman. "Overcoming Logistics Challenges in East Africa." *Army Sustainment* (January-February 2014): 28-31.

Klinger, Bruce. "The U.S. Should Support New South Korean President's Approach to North Korea." *Backgrounder* 2789 (April 11, 2013): 1.

Lata, Leenco. "The Ethiopia-Eritrea War: The Horn of Conflict." *Review of African Political Economy* 30, no. 97 (September 2003): 369-88.

Lee, Hong Yung. "North Korea in 2012: Kim Jong Un's Succession." *Asian Survey* 53, no. 1 (January/February 2013): 176-83.

Lerner, Mitchell "'Mostly Propaganda in Nature': Kim Il Sung, the Juche Ideology, and the Second Korean War." *Woodrow Wilson International Center for Scholars: North Korea International Documentation Project* 1, no. 3 (December 2010): 1-102.

Liddick, Jay, and David Anderson. "State Department/Coordinator for Reconstruction and Stabilization: Inception, Challenges, and Impact on U.S. Reconstruction and Stabilization Capacity." *Interagency Paper* 4, no. 1 (April 2011).

Lim, Jae-Cheon. "North Korea's Hereditary Succession." *Asian Survey* 52, no. 3 (June 2012): 550-570. http://dx.doi.org/10.1525/as.2012.52.3.550 (accessed October 17, 2013).

Lischer, Sarah. "Military Intervention and the Humanitarian 'Force Multiplier'." *Global Governance* 13, no. 1 (January-March 2007): 99-118.

Lloyd, John. "North Korea's Known Unknowns." Reuters. April 8, 2013. http://blogs.reuters.com/john-lloyd/2013/04/08/north-koreas-known-unknowns/ (accessed February 6, 2014).

McCormick, Shon. "A Primer On Developing Measures of Effectiveness." *Military Review* 90, no. 4 (July-August 2010): 60-66.

Medalia, Jonathan. *North Korea's 2009 Nuclear Test: Containment, Monitoring, Implications.* Washington, DC: Congressional Research Service, November 24, 2010.

Merriam, Sharan B. *Qualitative Research: a Guide to Design and Implementation.* 3rd ed. San Francisco: Jossey-Bass, 2009.

Minear, Larry. *The Humanitarian Enterprise: Dilemmas and Discoveries.* Bloomfield, CT: Kumarian Press, 2002.

National Committee on American Foreign Policy, "North Korea," *American Foreign Policy Interests* 29, no. 1 (2007): 87-90. http://dx.doi.org/10.1080/10803920601188201 (accessed October 17, 2013).

Nelson, Richard. *How Should NATO Handle Stabilization Operations and Reconstruction Efforts?* Washington, DC: Atlantic Council of the United States: Program on International Security, 2006.

Nikitin, Mary Beth. *North Korea's Nuclear Weapons: Technical Issues.* Washington, DC: Congressional Research Service, April 3, 2013.

Oleinik, Anton. "Mixing Quantitative and Qualitative Content Analysis: Triangulation at Work." *Quality and Quantity* 45, no. 4 (June 2011): 859-73. http://search.proquest.com/docview/861799694?accountid=12964.

Oliver, Ian. *War and Peace in the Balkans: The Diplomacy of Conflict in the Former Yugoslavia.* London: I.B. Tauris, 2005.

Paine, S. C. M. *The Sino-Japanese War of 1894-1895: Perceptions, Power, and Primacy.* Cambridge, England: Cambridge University Press, 2005.

Park, Han S., ed. *North Korea: Ideology, Politics, Economy.* Englewood Cliffs, NJ: Prentice Hall College Div, 1996.

Pate, Steven. *Transforming Logistics: Joint Theater Logistics.* Carlisle, PA: U.S. Army War College, 2006.

Patton, Michael Quinn. *Qualitative Research and Evaluation Methods.* 3rd ed. Thousand Oaks, CA: SAGE Publications, Inc, 2002.

Pausewang, Siegfried. "Eritrea: A Dream Deferred." *Forum for Development Studies* 37, no. 3 (November 2010): 415-16. http://dx.doi.org/10.1080/08039410.2010. 512416 (accessed January 28, 2014).

Pryce, Michael. *Improving S/CRS Planning Framework from a Geographic Combatant Command's Perspective: Analysis for Civil-Military Transitions.* Boiling Springs, PA: The Cornwallis Group XI, 2005.

Raugh, Harold Jr. *Operation Joint Endeavor: V Corps in Bosnia-Herzegovina 1995-1996, an Oral History.* Fort Leavenworth, KS: Combat Studies Institute Press, 2010.

Rotberg, Robert I. *Battling Terrorism in the Horn of Africa.* Cambridge, MA: World Peace Foundation, 2005.

Russell, Dawn, and John Saldanha. "Five Tenets of Security-Aware Logistics and Supply Chain Operation." *Transportation Journal* 42, no. 4 (Summer 2003): 44-54.

Sandler, Stanley. *The Korean War: No Victors, No Vanquished.* Lexington: The University Press of Kentucky, 1999.

Schaefer, Bernd. *Overconfidence Shattered: North Korean Unification Policy, 1971-1975.* Washington, DC: North Korea International Documentation Project: Woodrow Wilson International Center for Scholars, December 2010.

Schmidt, John R. "Can Outsiders Bring Democracy to Post-Conflict States?" *Orbis* 52, no. 1 (January 2008): 107-22. http://dx.doi.org/10.1016/j.orbis.2007.10.008 (accessed April 28, 2014).

Schuller, Mark and Pablo Morales. *Tectonic Shifts: Haiti Since the Earthquake.* Sterling, Va.: Kumarian Press, 2012.

Shrader, Charles R. *Communist Logistics in the Korean War.* Westport, CT: Greenwood Press, 1995.

Snyder, Scott. *Strengthening the U.S.-ROK Alliance.* Center for U.S.-Korea Policy: The Asia Foundation, February 2009.

Sofaer, S. "Qualitative Research Methods." *International Journal for Quality in Health Care* 14, no. 4 (August 2002): 329-36. http://dx.doi.org/10.1093/intqhc/14.4.329. (accessed January 28, 2014).

Soh, C. Sarah. "In/fertility among Korea's "comfort women" survivors: A comparative perspective." *Women's Studies International Forum* 29, no. 1 (January 2006): 67-80. http://dx.doi.org/10.1016/j.wsif.2005.10.007 (accessed April 28, 2014).

Steinberg, J. B., and Ford Foundation. *The Role of European Institutions in Security after the Cold War: Some Lessons from Yugoslavia*: Santa Monica, CA: Rand, 1992.

Styan, David. "Djibouti: Changing Influence in the Horn's Strategic Hub." In "Chatham House: AFP BP 2013/01." Special issue, *Chatham House Briefing Papers* (April 2013).

Suh, Hee-Kyung "Atrocities Before And During The Korean War." *Critical Asian Studies* 42, no. 4 (December 2010): 553-588. http://dx.doi.org/10.1080/14672715.2010.515388 (accessed October 17, 2013).

Suri, Harsh. "Purposeful Sampling in Qualitative Research Synthesis." *Qualitative Research Journal* 11, no. 2 (2011): 63-75. http://dx.doi.org/10.3316/QRJ1102063 (accessed January 28, 2014.

Szayna, Thomas, Derek Eaton, and Amy Richardson. *Preparing the Army for Stability Operations: Doctrinal and Interagency Issues*. Santa Monica, CA: Rand, 2007.

Teddlie, Charles, and Abbas Tashakkori. *Foundations of Mixed Methods Research: Integrating Quantitative and Qualitative Approaches in the Social and Behavioral Sciences*. Los Angeles: SAGE Publications, Inc., 2009.

The Asia Foundation, *North Korea Contingency Planning and U.S.-ROK Cooperation.* Washington, DC: Center for U.S.-Korea Policy, September 2009.

The Huffington Post, "North Korea Skating Close to a Dangerous Line, Says U.S. Defense Secretary Chuck Hagel," April 10, 2013. http://www.huffingtonpost.com/2013/04/10/north-korea-skating-close-dangerous-line-us-defense-secretary-chuck-hagel_n_3054533.html (accessed November 11, 2013).

The University of North Carolina-Chapel Hill. "What Happened to Yugoslavia? the War, the Peace and the Future: Examining Nato and the Evolution of the Trans-Atlantic Relationship." *Center for European Studies UNC– Chapel Hill* (Fall 2004): 1-16.

The White House, *National Security Strategy.* Washington, DC: The White House, May 2010.

———. *U.S. Strategy toward Sub-Saharan Africa.* Washington, DC: The White House, June 2012.

Tibbetts, John. *Power Projection Logistics: What Theater Support Unit?* Fort Leavenworth, KS: United States Army Command and General Staff College, 1995.

U.S. Army Command and General Staff College. Student Text 4-1, *Theater Sustainment Battle Book.* Fort Leavenworth, KS: U.S. Army Command and General Staff College, June 2013.

U.S. Department of the Army, Field Manual 4-40, *Quartermaster Operations.* Washington, DC: U.S. Department of the Army, October, 2013.

U.S. Joint Chiefs of Staff. Joint Publication 1-02, *Department of Defense Dictionary of Military and Associated Terms.* Washington, DC: U.S. Joint Chiefs of Staff, March 2014.

————. Joint Publication 3-0, *Joint Operations.* Washington, DC: U.S. Joint Chiefs of Staff, April 2011.

————. Joint Publication 4-0, *Joint Logistics.* Washington, DC: U.S. Joint Chiefs of Staff, October 2013.

U.S. Office of the Secretary of Defense. *Military and Security Developments Involving the Democratic People's Republic of Korea (A Report to Congress Pursuant to the National Defense Authorization Act for Fiscal Year 2012).* Washington, DC: Government Printing Office, 2012. http://www.defense.gov/pubs/ report_to_congress_on_military_and_security_developments_involving_the_dprk .pdf (accessed January 29, 2014).

U.S. Southern Command. *Operation Unified Response: First 100 Days (January 13-April 23, 2010).* Miami, FL: U.S. Southern Command Fact Sheet, April 23, 2010.

————. "Operation Unified Response: Support to Haiti Earthquake Relief 2010" http://www.southcom.mil/newsroom/Pages/Operation-Unified-Response-Support-to-Haiti-Earthquake-Relief-2010.aspx (accessed May 4, 2014).

United States Army Europe (USAREUR), *Military Operations: the U.S. Army in Bosnia and Herzegovina,* AE Pamphlet 525-100. Heidelberg, Germany: U.S. Army Europe and Seventh Army, October 7, 2003.

United States Department of State. *Post-Conflict Reconstruction Essential Tasks.* Washington, DC: U.S. Government Printing Office, April 2005. http://pksoi. army.mil/doctrine_concepts/documents/SCRC%20and%20J7/SCRS%20PCR%20 Essential%20Tasks%205%201%202005.pdf (accessed April 29, 2014).

Volman, Daniel. *Obama, AFRICOM, and U.S. Military Policy Toward Africa: Pas Working Paper Number 14.* Evanston, IL: Daniel Volman, 2009.

Waddell, Steve. *United States Army Logistics: From the American Revolution to 9/11.* Santa Barbara: Greenwood Publishing Group, 2010.

Walsh, Shawn P. "Bulk Fuel Support in Bosnia." *Army Logistician* 31, no. 4 (July/August 1999): 4. http://www.alu.army.mil/alog/issues/JulAug99/MS436.htm (accessed May 13, 2014).

Wassenhove, L. N. "Humanitarian Aid Logistics: Supply Chain Management in High Gear." *The Journal of the Operational Research Society* 57, no. 5 (May 2006): 475-89.

Wentz, Larry K. *Lessons from Bosnia: The IFOR Experience*. Honolulu, HI: University Press of the Pacific, 2002.

Whalen, Ryan. "The U.S. Government as an Interagency Network." *Interagency Journal* 4, no. 1 (Winter 2013): 75.

Wolf, Charles. *Straddling Economics and Politics: Cross-Cutting Issues in Asia, the United States, and the Global Economy.* Santa Monica, CA: Rand, 2002. http://www.rand.org/publications/mr/mr1571/ (accessed May 5, 2014).

Woodward, Peter. *US Foreign Policy and the Horn of Africa*. US Foreign Policy and Conflict in the Islamic World. Aldershot, Hants, England: Ashgate Pub. Co., 2006.

Wreszin, Michael. "The Korean War: A History," *American Communist History* 10, no. 3 (December 2011): 329-332. http://dx.doi.org/10.1080/14743892.2011.604490 (accessed October 17, 2013).

Young, Huh Moon. *Basic Reading on Korean Unification*. Seoul, Republic of Korea: Korea Institute for National Unification (KINU), 2012.

www.ingramcontent.com/pod-product-compliance
Lightning Source LLC
Chambersburg PA
CBHW080251290526
45790CB00005B/1767